4/20

D0195548

SCRIPTURE DISCUSSION COMMENTARY 6

Series editor: Laurence Bright

Psalms and Wisdom

Psalms *Leonard Johnston*

The wisdom literature *Michael Smith*

1972

248 pp

ACTA Foundation
Adult Catechetical Teaching Aids
Chicago, Illinois

First published 1972

ACTA Foundation (Adult Catechetical Teaching Aids), 4848 N. Clark Street
Chicago, Illinois 60640

Nihil obstat : John M. T. Barton, STD LSS   *Censor*
Imprimatur : + Victor Guazzelli   *Vicar General*
Westminster, 30 May 1972

Library of Congress number 71–173033

ISBN 0 87946 005 9

Made and printed in Great Britain by
William Clowes & Sons, Limited
London, Beccles and Colchester

Contents

v

General Introduction

A few of the individual units which make up this series of biblical commentaries have already proved their worth issued as separate booklets. Together with many others they are now grouped together in a set of twelve volumes covering almost all the books of the old and new testaments—a few have been omitted as unsuitable to the general purpose of the series.

That purpose is primarily to promote discussion. This is how these commentaries differ from the others that exist. They do not cover all that could be said about the biblical text, but concentrate on the features most likely to get lively conversation going—those, for instance, with special relevance for later developments of thought, or for life in the church and world of today. For this reason passages of narrative are punctuated by sets of questions designed to get a group talking, though the text of scripture, helped by the remarks of the commentator, should have already done just that.

For the text is what matters. Individuals getting ready for a meeting, the group itself as it meets, should always have the bible centrally present, and use the commentary only as a tool. The bibliographies will help those wishing to dig deeper.

What kinds of group can expect to work in this way?

Absolutely any. The bible has the reputation of being difficult, and in some respects it is, but practice quickly clears up a lot of initial obstacles. So parish groups of any kind can and should be working on it. The groups needn't necessarily already exist; it is enough to have a few like-minded friends and to care sufficiently about finding out what the Bible means. Nor need they be very large; one family could be quite enough. High schools (particularly in the senior year), colleges and universities are also obvious places for groups to form. If possible they should everywhere be ecumenical in composition: though all the authors are Roman catholics, there is nothing sectarian in their approach.

In each volume there are two to four or occasionally more studies of related biblical books. Each one is self-contained; it is neither necessary nor desirable to start at the beginning and plough steadily through. Take up, each time, what most interests you—there is very little in scripture that is actually dull! Since the commentaries are by different authors, you will discover differences of outlook, in itself a matter of discussion. Above all, remember that getting the right general approach to reading the bible is more important than answering any particular question about the text—and that this approach only comes with practice.

Volume six contains the psalms, written and collected over a long period of time, and the wisdom writings, amongst the last of the old testament period. The psalms are collected under themes, and a selection only of wisdom is commented, in order to keep the volume to a reasonable length.

L. B.

The psalms

Leonard Johnston

Introduction

One of the most striking things about the psalms, from a literary point of view, is their variety. They are a collection of poems or hymns by different authors, from different dates, in different situations (none of them known with any certainty), of very varying merit and on a variety of subjects. Of none of the psalms can it be said simply that it deals with this subject in this way. Any attempt to group them into categories comes up against this difficulty. Some of them are laments, for example; but it may be a lament for sin, or for some setback like a failure of the harvest, or for a great national disaster like a defeat in battle. Or if you decide to take the subject of sin, some of the psalms are pathetic laments for the suffering which sin has brought about, some of them are the powerful condemnation of the prophets, some of them may be didactic moralising.

The one thing all the psalms have in common is that they are 'biblical'. The bible itself is a vast, unwieldy collection of literature; and the psalms are 'the mirror of the bible in prayer'. The bible is 'the word of God'; it is the expression of Israel's consciousness of the action of God in the world, in history, in their own national life and its institutions. In all of these God spoke to them (and through them to us). The psalms are their reaction to that word; in all

3

these ways God communicated with them, and this is their response; it is their experience transmuted into prayer.

This may explain the principle behind the pages which follow. It is not a verse-by-verse commentary on the text of individual psalms; but then the psalms are not primarily meant to be read with a commentary, any more than one says the Lord's prayer with one eye on a commentary. The psalms are meant to be prayed. But since what gives them their value is the fact that they are the word of God, then what we need is a mind full of the bible which forms the very substance of these prayers. Here then is an outline of the main ideas which run through the whole psalter, with a brief comment on some of the psalms in which these ideas occur. This may leave untouched some minor and incidental obscurities in the text; but if these ideas colour and mould our own thinking as we pray the psalms, then there is a chance that our minds will be in tune with that of the writer— and with that of the Holy Spirit.

The numbering is that of the Hebrew psalter, as seen in the Revised Standard Version.

Book list

A. Weiser, *The Psalms* (SCM, 1962).

H. Ringgren, *The Faith of the Psalmist* (SCM, 1963).

T. Worden, *The Psalms are Christian Prayer* (Chapman, 1963).

D. Anders-Richards, *The Drama of the Psalms* (DLT, 1968).

1

The great deeds of God

History as revelation

If the psalms are the summing up of the whole bible in the form of prayer, then it is not surprising that history should play a large part in them; for history provides the shape and pattern of the whole bible. The events of Israel's past are the basis for praise of God's greatness and goodness (as in psalms 68 and 114), confession of Israel's guilt (as in 77 and 79) and an appeal to his mercy (as in 44, 60 and 80). But sometimes the story of the past is simply narrated, almost for its own sake; and this can cause some difficulty to us, twentieth-century readers—a history lesson proposed to us as a prayer.

The first and most basic fact that we must bear in mind is that in the bible history is revelation. When we use the word 'revelation' today we are inclined to think of the content of revelation, the doctrine or truth which is revealed; the real presence is a revelation, that there are three persons in the one God is a revelation. But the important thing about revelation is not *what* is revealed but the fact that it has taken place—that God has made himself known to us, that he has entered into communication with us; that we are not left to our own devices (our own reason or imagination) in our search for God or, to put it

5

the other way round, that the God we are dealing with is not simply the product of our minds or the projection of our own hopes and desires, but that he really exists, outside of us and independent of us, and that he has come to us, we have not invented him.

This communication can and does take place in many ways—through the phenomena of the created world, for example, or through conscience—but Israel's faith is that it also takes place in a series of historical events. This does not mean that the drama of human history is an illusion, and that behind the apparent interplay of free agents there is an inexorable power manipulating men like puppets. But it does mean that human life is more than it seems; it is a drama in which God himself is involved. Life is meaningful.

This becomes clearer when we consider the view of life implied in paganism, or in an 'atheist' philosophy. For the pagans amongst whom Israel's faith was born, the gods were personifications of the forces at work in human life. Theology is mythology—stories which dramatise or caricature the lives of the gods representing natural phenomena. But Israel was aware of a god who was 'other'—who was not simply a personification of natural forces but who was different in kind from all that our world contains. Sometimes this difference is expressed in terms of physical remoteness: 'His glory is above the heavens—seated on high, he needs to stoop to see the sky and earth' (113:5). But the one thing it does not mean is real remoteness: 'The wicked say: The Lord does not see. He who planted the ear, does he not hear? He who formed the eye, does he not see?' (94:7 f). 'The Lord's throne is in heaven, his eyes behold the children of men' (11:4). This is in fact the essential difference between Israel's God and any other: 'Their idols have eyes but never see, ears but never hear, feet but never walk' (115: 5–7); whereas Israel's God is the God whose will is supreme in the heavens and on the earth (115:3); who has not eyes or hands like ours, like those attributed to an idol, but who is both aware of what men do and is involved in their actions.

God is at work in our lives, it is here that he communicates with us. He communicates also in our conscience, in our reason, in our hearts. But if these were the only ways in which God communicated with us, it would imply that the only important element in religion is the relationship between God and the individual human soul. Stories about his supposed activity in our world would be irrelevant except as illustrating the sort of God we are thinking of. It would be quite legitimate and indeed necessary to 'demythologise' such stories in order to make clear the only thing of importance—the relationship between God and the individual human soul. Israel's faith in a God of history makes it clear that what is involved is not merely the mind of man but the existence of the world.

God reveals himself to us in history; history is the situation in which God communicates with us. The 'word of God' is not simply a statement; it is a deed, and a deed of power, a deed in which God's very being is involved, offering himself to us and calling for our response: 'As the rain and snow come down from the heavens and do not return without watering the earth, making it yield and giving growth to provide seed for the sower and bread for the eating, so the word that goes from my mouth does not return to me empty, without carrying out my will' (Is 55: 10 f). And in the same way, to 're-member' God's great deeds is not simply a passive, subjective activity. In the act of remembering, God's power-

ful, demanding word is made available to us today, now.
God has communicated with men in history, and by remembering—reliving—this event, we enter into that
communication.

But when we say that God has revealed himself in history, we mean more specifically in *this* history, the history
conveyed to us by the bible. We are not just saying that
God is at work in the world, so that with enough in-
genuity or imagination or piety we may discern signs of
his activity. Why is this? Why, for example, do we treat
the account of Israel's battles with the Assyrians as
'sacred history', and not Caesar's *Gallic War*?

There are two considerations which make Israel's history different from any other. First, it is at least arguable
that Israel's history was not in fact any different from
any other—that God was no more 'with them' than he
was with, say, the Egyptians. That God is the Lord of all
men is certainly true, and Israel recognises this: 'I will
add Egypt and Babylon to the nations that acknowledge
me' (87:4): 'The leaders of the nations rally to the people
of the God of Abraham. Every shield in the world belongs to God, he reigns supreme' (47:9). One might then
say that the difference is not in the way in which God
deals with different peoples, but in Israel's awareness of
his action. When we remember the great deeds of God,
it is not so much a special category of actions that we are
remembering, but we are making Israel's faith and praise
our own.

Nevertheless, it is true that this particular series of ac-
tions has a term; they lead up to the great deed of God in
our Lord Jesus Christ. Jesus of Nazareth was not an
Egyptian or a Babylonian; he was 'son of David, son of
Abraham', as the new testament genealogies point out.
He is the climax of that history, and it is this which for a

christian validates the history. He is the word of God—the word which spoke in different ways at various times became flesh in Jesus (Heb 1:1-4, Jn 1:14). It is this which gives meaning and value to the history of Israel. It is like a train going through a tunnel; we not only glimpse the daylight which lies ahead at the end of the tunnel, but this light shines into the tunnel itself. It is therefore legitimate and even necessary for a christian to read the account of God's great deeds with full awareness of its full and final meaning in Christ.

What then are we doing as we put before ourselves in prayer the events of Israel's past? First, we are expressing our faith in a transcendent God, one who exists independently of our own minds. Secondly, we are proclaiming our faith that human life and human history are meaningful; not in the sense that the past has lessons for us, nor in the sense that it is a pattern of allegories in which our timeless relation with God is represented; but in the sense that human life is the situation in which a personal God is with us, and in which we as persons respond to him. Thirdly, we recognise a specific series of events in which God's love and mercy entered human life, and in prayer we embrace this salvation and make it our own. But finally, we do so always 'in Christ': we realise that whenever God comes to man, he does so in his word—his word who finally became flesh, and who shared with us his Spirit. The history of Israel is a 'sacrament' by which we enter into dialogue with the Triune God who is our life.

Ps 105

Most of the historical references in the psalms are to the exodus, with which the next section will deal; some contain incidental references to specific incidents (like the free account of incidents from the book of Judges in 68: 12–23, or the recalling of ancient victories in 83:6–12). But 78, 105, 106 and 107 are examples of psalms almost entirely devoted to historical narrative. We may take psalm 105 as a typical example.

It begins (105:1–6) with a heartfelt summons to praise the Lord, to exult in his holy name (3). He is holy; he is totally beyond our reach; and how could we know him if he had not made himself known to us? We could know *about* God, we could know the idea of deity; but we could not really reach him if he had not come to us. We are not dealing with the God of philosophy, or a God about whom we may speak eternal and timeless truths, or a God who is known only in the silence and mystery of the individual, secret human soul. Our God is one whom we know in his deeds.

And our song of praise, our 'remembering' (5), is not just a mental projection into the past. His strength is not ended by any specific deed; he did not withdraw himself after making himself known in these incidents. This same God is still with us now; through the recollection of the past we encounter him now. We 'seek the Lord and his strength continually' (4). 7–15 recalls briefly the story of the patriarchs, Abraham especially. For it was there that the story began which still determines our lives today—a story of free grace; choice, covenant, promise. It is these which make it possible for us to call him 'our' God (7); through us his will is known in the world (7)— not an inscrutable mystery hidden in the heavens. Through us the good news that we have a loving God, a merciful God, a saving God, is proclaimed to all men (1), known in all the earth (7). Yet, though it is for all men, those who handed on this message—and those who do so today—are favoured of God, they are 'anointed', they are prophets (15).

16–22 then give a free version of the story of Joseph: bringing out the strange changes of fortunes in his story in order to bring out the unchanging but mysterious mercy of God. We then have a similar version of the events surrounding the exodus (23–42).

The events at Mount Sinai are a notable omission. Perhaps this is because the occasion when the psalm was meant to be sung was an occasion like that of Deut 26:1–10—the occasion of a harvest festival, an occasion for thanksgiving for the land which God has given them and its fruits. This too is why it ends (43–45) with the possession of the promised land—the land in which the Israelites who were called on to sing the hymn still lived; the blessings which are ours, we who pray with them.

1. Does the idea of 'God in history' make any difference to our understanding of history? Is the 'message' clear, or is it ambiguous? Does this then suggest any reflexion on the meaning of 'words'? Are they meant primarily to convey a clear message?

2. What ideas does this psalm suggest about the nature of God's action in the world?

2

Our God, our saviour

The first and decisive event in Israel's history was the exodus. In the psalms, the importance of this event is reflected not so much in the number of psalms devoted to it directly (like 105, 106, 114) as in the fact that it determines almost the whole of Israel's thought and in one way or another underlies all the psalms.

It is convenient to sum up all that should be said about the exodus under two heads; the meaning of the name 'Yahweh'—what Israel thought about their God; and the institution of the covenant—Israel's relationship with God.

Yahweh

Israelite tradition links the origin of the name 'Yahweh' with the liberation from Egypt. When Moses received the commission to lead the people to freedom, he was told that the name of the God who sent him was 'I am who I am', Yahweh (Ex 3:13–15).

This is the same sort of narrative as that found earlier in the explanation of the name of Moses himself. The real meaning of the word 'Moses' is something like 'born of'— it is found as a component of such Egyptian names as Ra-moses or Tut-moses; but some similarity with the Hebrew verb 'to take' enabled the writer to attach it to the legend of Moses' birth and interpret it as meaning 'taken from the waters'. So here, the real origin and meaning of the name 'Yahweh' is not known to the author or certainly not of any interest to him; but through a plausible similarity with the Hebrew verb 'to be' it is interpreted as 'I am who I am'.

This may be seen in the first place as a rejection of Moses' request to know the name. In the ancient world, the gods like everything and everyone else had their own proper names, Baal, Marduk, Isis and so on. Names were much more than a convenient way of labelling a person. The name expresses the reality of a person; until you know his name he does not exist for you; and equally to know the name is to have a grasp of the person, to have him to some extent in your power. All names were 'names to conjure with'; to call on the name is to summon the person to your assistance.

Israel's God has not a name like that. He simply 'is'. By calling their God 'Yahweh', 'he who is', the Israelites proclaimed their recognition that he was not the sort of person who can be grasped, totally comprehended, at man's beck and call and subject to his control. It denotes what we would call 'transcendence', what the bible would call 'holiness'. The Hebrew word which is usually translated 'holy' means cut off, separate, distinct, different, other. It expresses an awareness that there is more to our world and life than can be explained in purely human terms; that besides our world, behind or beyond it, there is something other—a reality, a power, a presence. In its most primitive stage, this may be seen simply as man's reaction to a world which is in so many ways mysterious to him, which in so many ways—sickness, death, or even the succession of the seasons—falls outside his control. It is an emotive term, expressing awe and terror at the *mysterium tremendum et fascinosum*. But for Israel this emotive term developed a genuinely ontological meaning: the awareness of a God who while being completely different from anything which lies within our world is yet completely personal; who from beyond our world freely 'intervenes'. I put 'intervenes' in inverted commas because this is not the only way of describing God's relationship with our world, nor even the best way. As the bible itself is clearly aware and as we shall see later, God and his action is also to be found within our world.

Yahweh, the God who is, is not a figment of the imagination, not a personification of their own dreams or desires or hopes or fears. He really is; and you know a person by his actions. Israel's God is 'other', holy; but not for this reason completely detached from us. He acts, and he is experienced in his actions. This is the basis of Israel's concept of revelation, and indeed the beginning of a concept of history. Events do not occur in a fixed cycle nor yet as a meaningless sequence of incidents. In the events of human history there is a living, personal will —Yahweh who is.

He really is, unlike the idols which the bible likes to describe as 'vanity', emptiness, nothingness, unreal, with no reality beyond the imagination of the craftsman who made them or the worshipper who gives them honour. 'They have hands, but cannot touch, eyes but cannot see.' This common jibe in the bible is quite crude as apologetic; for surely the idolators too were as aware as the Israelites of the man-made origin of their statues. But the Israelites were really more concerned with saying what God is, than with what the idols are not: 'The idols of silver and gold have mouths but never speak, eyes that

never see . . . But I know that the Lord is great, whatever
he pleases he does, in heaven, and on earth; he raises
up clouds and makes the lightning flash' (135:15–16,
5–7).

Israel was forbidden to make any idol to represent
Yahweh. This was not only to mark the difference between him and any other idea of divinity, but also because for the God who is 'other', non-representation is the
best representation of him. He is a hidden God, whom
our eyes cannot see, but who makes himself known to us
in his actions. It was in their history, not in a graven
image, that Israel encountered their God.

The same body of ideas also lies behind the bible's use
of anthropomorphic language. God laughs with scorn
(2:4); God's fingers set the stars in place (8:4); God
smites his enemies on the jaw (3:7), and so on. These are
not strictly figures of speech, nor are they really a weakness of language. They are effective expressions of the
vital reality of the living God which is concealed and
killed by the inert formulae of philosophy. This is particularly true of the 'miraculous' element which plays
such a large part in the bible, especially in the account
of the exodus. The 'phenomena' which accompany the
events at Mount Sinai—the thunder, the lightning, the
mountain wreathed with smoke—these express the shock
and disruption of the God who is 'other' coming into contact with our world. 'What is it makes you take to flight,
O sea, or Jordan turn back? Why do the mountains
skip like rams or the hills like little lambs? Tremble,
earth, at the coming of your master' (114:5–7).
When the almighty comes into the world, the total
upset of the established order is natural; the water turns
to dry land (114:3), and the dry land turns to water
(114:8).

Covenant

God came to Israel in the great event of the exodus; but
this event established a bond between themselves and
Yahweh, which they called a covenant. The form in
which this was expressed followed the pattern of the political treaties of the day, especially the so-called 'suzer-
ainty treaties' which an overlord granted to a vassal.
Such treaties begin with the title of the suzerain and a
reminder of the historical events which have put his vas-
sals under obligation ('I am Yahweh who brought you
out of Egypt'). Then the stipulations of the treaty are laid
down (Israel's laws), including the obligation to refrain
from alliance with any of the king's enemies ('Thou shalt
not have other gods besides me'). Then a series of blessings and curses are attached to the keeping or breaking
of the treaty (Lev 26 or Deut 28 give the biblical version
of this). And finally a copy of the treaty is to be deposited
in the shrine of the god (as Israel's law was placed in the
ark of the covenant).

Israel, then, recognised Yahweh as their sovereign
lord. His will is their law. The actual 'laws' were of
course drawn from many different sources and develop
under the same sort of influences as any other body of
law; but Israel regarded them as expressing the will of
God who had chosen them as his own.

But the relationship lay much deeper than a purely
legal relationship. For the exodus on which it was
founded was an act of deliverance, a salvation, an act of
mercy and of gratuitous love. The legal concept of a political treaty therefore was not the only way to express it;
it was also a marriage bond, a betrothal. Israel was the
bride of Yahweh, and was called to much more than
formal obedience to the stipulations of a treaty: 'Hear, O

Israel. Yahweh is God alone; and you shall love Yahweh with your whole heart and soul and strength' (Deut 6:4 f). To break the treaty was not just the disloyalty of a vassal, but adultery, a breach of marriage vows, and the punishment it evoked was the jealousy of an offended lover. 'How much longer will you be angry, Yahweh—how long will your jealousy blaze like a fire?' (79:5).

And there was even more than this. The covenant not only determined the national way of life; it even brought them into existence as a nation. Israel is often described, in a conventional formula, as 'the sons of Jacob', as if the nation were simply the descendants of the patriarchs arrived at national status by the normal process of reproduction. But this is a simplification, as the bible itself shows. Elements of many different ethnic and cultural groups went to make up Israel: 'Your origin and birth are of the land of the Canaanites; your father was an Amorite and your mother a Hittite' (Ez 16:3). There were people of different tribes and races among them, and these are bound together not by common ancestry, but by alliance—by the covenant. Without the covenant, then, there was no such thing as Israel, there was only a motley group of peoples. Because of the covenant, they were indeed 'the people of God'. This means that Israel can never be motivated simply by patriotism; nor can religion be for them merely the expression of the *genius populi*. The nation exists for God.

For them to call God 'Father' was not simply the common recognition of a God who brings all things into existence. It expressed the specific relationship of a people who owed their very existence as a nation to his saving and creative act. He was their father, they were his sons—his first-born son. The land which they called 'the promised land', was theirs by right of inheritance, theirs as sons and heirs.

Yahweh is their God, and they are his people. They are bound in union. God is no longer simply 'other'. The chasm has been bridged, the absolute and total barrier which separates us from God has been broken down. He is no longer 'other'; he is 'one of us', he is on our side. He is not remote, objective, a power coldly considering and judging our actions from afar. He is 'with us', he is for us. Like any other nation, Israel strove for security and prosperity; but as the people of God they expected these things, as covenant blessings.

This does not mean that God has ceased to be God. He is still the holy one; but Israel has been assumed into the sphere of the holy—they are a holy people. The name of God—the holy name, expressing his being which is not bound—has been laid on Israel in trust for the world.

The exodus and the psalms

Clearly, the exodus is much more than a specific topic to be noted in individual psalms. It underlies almost all the psalms, and colours the language and thought so deeply that it is difficult to limit the examples.

We have already mentioned how Israel's experience of the exodus gives a very specific note to their use of the word 'Father' applied to God; for them it means not only the care which he has for all that he has brought into being, but his particular role in their regard—without him, the nation would not exist. This in turn, as we have also seen, gives rise to the idea of 'inheritance': that Israel, as God's sons, has a right to his blessings, especially the land which he promised them. With this too is connected the word 'saviour' when it is used as a translation of the Hebrew word *go'el*. The *go'el* is the next of kin who has certain family responsibilities. The best known form of this is the law of levirate, by which the *go'el*, the next of kin, is expected to marry a deceased relative's widow so as to ensure the continuance of the line. The *go'el* too ensured justice for a murdered man by bringing vengeance on his murderer. God was Israel's next of kin, her *go'el*, her saviour, who would ensure her life and honour even in the face of death.

The covenant was also a marriage bond; God was Israel's spouse, she was his bride, and this view of their relationship gave it a deep emotional content.

How exactly the escape from Egypt was accomplished is not really known, but it was certainly not by force of arms of the Israelites; and yet it was a great victory in which the Egyptians were defeated. God was the victor; 'with mighty arm and outstretched hand' he led his people to freedom. And in all their later battles they would call on their warrior God to fight on their behalf; to appeal to the God of battles, to summon him 'to take his sword and shield, to brandish lance and spear' (35:3), is to appeal to the God of the exodus.

'The Lord is my shepherd': but the occasion when God showed himself their shepherd was when 'he guided his people like a flock by the hands of Moses and Aaron' (77:20), led them through the desert, to the rich land of Canaan, and provided them with water on the way. They were themselves a semi-nomadic people at that time, living by herding flocks from oasis to oasis on the outskirts of the cultivated land; and this was the way they thought of themselves, as helpless and as lost as sheep; and this was the way they thought of their God, their shepherd. The reference in the mind of an Israelite was not primarily to the tender and emotional image it is liable to rouse in us;

it is primarily a historical reference—a reference to the God who 'led his people through the wilderness like a flock, who guided them safe and unafraid' (78:52).

In the pathless waste he led them safely as if on a highway; and 'the way' for them always had undertones of this journey. 'The journey of life' is a metaphor which is so trite as to be completely dead; and it is made even more colourless and inert in English by the fact that 'the way' can also mean a 'method', 'manner', 'custom'—a particular way of acting. (It may help to remember that this is not so in other languages. In French, 'une façon de parler' is quite different from 'une route'.) Many phrases in the psalms pass us by completely because of this: 'he teaches the way to sinners' (25:8) sounds as if it simply meant 'he shows them the right conduct'. It is true that often it has become a conventional term: 'Happy those who walk in the law of Yahweh' (119:1), so that there is some excuse for translations which render it by some word like 'intentions', or 'actions' or 'life'. But nearly always somewhere underlying 'the way' there is a reference to the experience of the exodus. Israel's life began with a journey, and their covenant with God was not merely internal or mental or spiritual; it involved doing something, going somewhere. 'The way of the Lord' was in the first place this journey from slavery to freedom, the journey to a promised land; a journey in which the route was not clearly laid out and sign-posted but on which God led them by a pillar of cloud by day and a fire by night; a way on which he himself provided them with food, as he did when he sent them manna or water from the rock; a way on which he protected them and would always protect them: 'He has given his angels charge over you to protect you in the way' (91:11). When later they were again in desperate need, in exile in Babylon, a prophet used the same language to promise salvation: 'Prepare in the desert the way of the Lord' (Is 40:3). It is a way of salvation, and also a way of revelation—it is on this way that God shows himself: 'The glory of the Lord will be revealed' (Is 40:5). It is, therefore, the way which God himself walks; it is a holy way and to follow him means being like him: 'it is a holy way, nothing defiled shall walk on it' (Is 35:8). But above all it is a way of mercy, a way of life; to abandon this way is to be lost in a pathless, waterless waste.

In the same context belongs the figure of 'the tree'. It is a graphic description of God's life-giving power that 'the desert will blossom like a rose' (Is 35:1); and Israel too had known that power—against all hope, against expectation it had grown in the desert, had sprung to life in that arid soil. She was like a tree planted by the waters, reaching out deep roots, standing firmly and rich in blossom and fruit (1:3). She is the vine planted by God, and transplanted to Canaan (80:8), which he protected and fostered and waited to fruit (Is 5:1–7).

One phrase above all seems to sum up the meaning of the covenant: 'grace and truth'—*hesed we'emeth*. The word *hesed* combines several meanings which no one word in English renders. It means love; not simply friendliness but not passionate love either; *agape* rather than *eros* (and *agape* is in fact one of the Greek words used to translate *hesed* in the new testament). It is a love like that of a mother for her child ('Can a mother forget her child, not remember the child she has born? Yet if she should forget, yet will I not forget thee', Is 49:15). It is a love which gives rather than receives; it is a love which is not evoked by any desirable quality in its object, but which rather bestows grace on that object. It is a love, therefore, which goes out particularly to those in need—

to the poor, the orphan, the widow, the oppressed, the wretched, the despised. It is also, then, mercy. It is this which Israel had experienced in the exodus when, through no merits of her own, unexpectedly, gratuitously, Yahweh had reached out and given her freedom and life, had lifted her up from the dung-hill and made her his bride.

Emeth means 'truth'; but not with the philosophic, intellectual connotation it has in Greek or in western thought generally. It has a pragmatic meaning—true as a note of music is true, true as a friend is true. It means reliable, trustworthy. The characteristic Greek metaphor for truth is light; in Hebrew it is the rock, the word so often applied to God. He is rock-like in his reliability, because he is rock-like in his reality. He was like the rocks that rose out of the desert that Israel passed through on their way from Egypt. You can't walk through a rock as if it were a mental concept or a mirage. And God was their rock, sure foothold in the shifting sands, shade from the deadly sun, defence against enemy attack, 'God, my strength, my rock, my bastion, my deliverer; I take shelter in him, my rock, my shield, my salvation' (18:1–2).

And God is true, reliable, because of his love; and he loves because this is the reality of his being. Other gods, or fate, may be beneficent, but not unfailingly; their favours are accidental or capricious. But Yahweh's love is as unfailing as his being. *Hesed we'emeth*: God's love is not a 'quality', but the very reality of his being; his love is true, trustworthy, because his truth, his reality, is love.

The christian psalms

'The law was given through Moses: grace and truth came through Jesus Christ' (Jn 1:17). A christian reader does not have to project himself into a historical past when he reads the psalms; the whole of the new testament so obviously speaks the language of the exodus that these psalms simply take on a richer pattern of meaning for us; they express our joy and gratitude and triumph, our hope and need and yearning, as really as they do for the psalmist.

The very word used to describe what Christ did for us is the same word as that used for the exodus, 'liberation'. His sacrifice was 'a new covenant', and by it God has come closer to us, 'dwelt amongst us'; he is 'for us'. 'If God be for us, who is against us' (Rom 8:31). He has made us a people; we who were once no people at all are now the people of God (1 Pet 2:10), a holy people, a new people sharing the same life; 'There is now no more Jew or gentile, slave or free, male or female, but we are all one in Christ' (Gal 3:28). In Christ, Israel's destiny as sons of God was completed, he was 'called out of Egypt to be God's son' (Mt 2:15); and we too are sons in him, called to the freedom of sons of God. As Israel passed through the Red Sea to freedom and life, he passed through the waters of death and we passed through the waters of baptism. They remember 'the way' across the desert to the promised land; but Christ says 'I am the way; he who follows me does not walk in darkness but has the light of life'. We follow him, he our good shepherd; and as we go we are fed with the true bread from heaven (Jn 6:32) and water from the rock which is Christ (1 Cor 10:4). Israel was the tree of God's planting; and Christ is the vine, and we are the branches.

No, we have no need to strain after allegories and subtle spiritual meanings. These psalms put on our lips a hymn of praise to the eternal love of God our saviour.

Ps 114

The exodus (using the term in a broad sense, to cover the liberation from Egypt, the journey through the desert and the events at Sinai) is so decisive for Israel's life and thought that in one way or another it enters into our understanding of nearly all the psalms. It adds a further dimension to even such a familiar poem as Ps 23. God's saving action may be described in terms reminiscent of this saving action (18:7–15 echoes the language of Sinai; 107:10–16 reminds us of the exodus). More directly, it forms part of the appeal to God's past mercies in 68, 77, 78 and 136. In 81, 106 and 114 it forms the substance of the psalm—as a subject for joyful praise, as a reminder of past infidelity, as a motive for renewed faithfulness.

Ps 114 is a brief hymn which manages to bring some poetic originality to the well-known theme. When Israel thinks about their role, their destiny, their national character, it is to the exodus that they look. They were brought out of Egypt not to national independence, but to be God's kingdom; not to find a home of their own, but to be his home. (It reminds one of what is said of wisdom in Sir 24:7–12; having been God's agent in creating the world and all its peoples, wisdom then seeks a home for herself, and is directed to this people: 'And so I was established in Zion, in the beloved city he gave me a resting place, in Jerusalem was my dominion'.) Through them the holy God was to be with men; through them his presence and power were to be operative in the world.

It was for this reason that Egypt was for them a foreign land. It was a country of great wealth, luxury and culture; it was a country where many wanderers from the desert settled down gratefully and happily. But Israel was 'set apart'; they were strangers and exiles (cf 1 Pet 2:4).

Israel was 'set apart', because God was 'set apart', holy (cf p 13). The same characteristic of God is seen too in other events recorded in the tradition from those days. The events are noted with mock astonishment (and with a touch of humour); but only to bring out (7 f) the reality underlying them. By his deliverance of Israel the holy God has come into the world of men; and when this happens, the 'natural' order is upset. Dry land becomes a spring you can drink from, water becomes something you can walk on; rivers flow backwards, the solid mountains skip like lambs—this is what it is like for the infinite and almighty God to come into our life; for the 'word' to become 'flesh'.

1. When looking at the 'exodus' imagery in the psalms mentioned in this chapter (eg 105, 106, 114) what do we understand about the action of God in the lives we live under the new covenant?

2. What does Ps 114 tell us about the purpose of redemption, and the role of the redeemed people?

3. What does this way of looking at the exodus suggest about the meaning of Mt 28:2 or 27:51?

3

Creator of heaven and earth

Heaven and earth

The psalms generally reflect the same world-picture as that presented in the first chapters of Genesis—an account of creation based on the way the world appears to natural, unscientific observation. The earth appears as a flat disk floating on water (waters which break out to produce seas and rivers and springs), with the sky stretched above it like a canopy; against this canopy are pinned the heavenly bodies like jewels or like lamps, and above it there is yet more water which leaks through as rain; and above all this again is the dwelling place of God. 'The Lord is in his holy palace, the Lord is enthroned in the heavens' (104:2), and from the storerooms there on high he pours out water on the earth (104:13).

This pictorial representation is a way of expressing certain ideas about God and his relationship to the world. (It is all the more important to be clear on this distinction, when our view of the world is so completely different.) It expresses first of all the idea of God's total supremacy—he is not part of our world, he is separate from it, he is 'other', and totally above it: 'Heaven is the Lord's—earth he has given to the sons of men' (115:16); 'As high as heaven is above the earth, so are my ways

26

above your ways' (Is 55:9). He is the ruler of the world:
'The Lord made the heavens, before him are splendour
and majesty, in his sanctuary are strength and beauty . . .
Adore the Lord in his holy place, tremble before him, all
the earth' (96:6–9).

But this does not mean that he is remote and uncon-
cerned. He notes all our actions: 'The Lord is enthroned
in the heavens, but his eyes behold the children of men'
(11:4). From heaven he sends down the waters that give
life to the earth (104:13); to heaven we look for help: 'I
lift up my eyes to the hills: whence comes my help?
Help comes to me from the Lord who made heaven and
earth' (121:1 f); 'To thee I lift my eyes, to thee enthroned in heaven' (123:1).

'Heaven' is not merely a symbol of height and separation from earth; covering the earth from end to end
(19:7), it is also a symbol of his nearness, of his continual
presence: 'As high as heaven is above the earth, so is your
love for those who fear you' (103:11).

This is one view of creation and one theology based on
it. But several passages of the bible have another way of
representing creation, one which is much closer to that
of the ancient mythologies. This view represents creation
as a great battle between the gods. In the Babylonian
myth, for example, the original state of the world was a
vast, formless, watery chaos in which the goddess of
ocean, Tiamat, ruled supreme. But against her comes
forth Marduk, the sun god, to challenge her dominion.
Tiamat summons various animal figures to assist her,
'viper, serpent, hound'; but Marduk is victorious.
He splits the body of Tiamat in two and sets up
one half as the heavens, where also he chains her
animal allies who become the figures of the constellations.

The battle of creation

References to such a primordial battle are found at various places in the bible. In the book of Job, Bildad praises God's almighty power:

> By his strength he stilled the sea
> By his wisdom he crushed Rahab,
> His breath made beautiful the heavens,
> His hand pierced the flying serpent (Job 26:12 f).

Rahab is a mythical being associated with the sea, perhaps identical with it (in Is 30:7 and Ps 87:4 the word is used for Egypt, stretched out by the Nile like a sea-serpent). Rahab, then, plays a part similar to that of Tiamat in the Babylonian myth; Job 9:13 speaks of God defeating 'the helpers of Rahab', as Marduk defeated Tiamat and her allies.

This Rahab is also associated with the sea, and with another monster called 'a dragon', in Is 51:9:

> Was it not thou that didst cut Rahab in pieces,
> That didst pierce the dragon?
> Was it not thou that didst dry up the sea?

And the sea, the dragon and the serpent (called Leviathan) are again together opposed to God in Is 27:1:

> In that day, the Lord will punish
> Leviathan, the fleeing serpent, Leviathan the twisting serpent,
> And will slay the dragon in the sea.

Israel, then, knows a myth very like that of Marduk and Tiamat, in which God is ranged against the sea, Rahab, Leviathan the serpent, and the dragon in the sea. And Job explicitly connects the taming of the sea with creation:

Where were you when I laid foundations of the
earth . . .
Who shut in the seas with doors when it burst forth,
Prescribed bounds for it, set bars and doors, and
said:
Thus far shall you come and no further,
Here shall your proud waves be stayed (Job 38:4–
11).

The psalms also speak of God 'bottling up the sea'
(33:7); the waters take to flight at God's rebuke (104:7),
God fixes a limit for the waters which they must not pass
(148:6).

These texts give a view of creation quite different from
that of Genesis, and quite similar to that of the myth—a
view of creation as the result of a victory won by God
over the opposing powers of the ocean and allied monsters. And as with the other view, this one too implies and
expresses a certain theology.

According to the myth and the biblical passages tribut-
ary to it, creation is described as a struggle. From a
philosophical point of view this idea, with its implication
of dualism, is no doubt less satisfactory than that of creation by a simple act of the divine will, by his word. But
such a view, intellectually acceptable though it may be,
does not convey anything of the emotional impact of
what is involved in creation; of the outpouring of the
divine being—his light, his order, his beauty where there
would otherwise be only the darkness of chaos or nothingness. Philosophically, of course, we recognise that
where there was non-God there was nothing at all—
there was simply nothingness. But to describe creation as
a struggle, as a victory over the forces of chaos, does
effectively convey the idea that God in creating takes
possession of an area where 'previously' he was absent;

creation is the assertion of a divine quality where 'previously' there was non-God.

Moreover, creation is not an isolated act, but a continuing process. It is a continual outpouring of the divine vitality, a continual assertion of being against the continual threat of non-being, symbolised by the waters of chaos. God has mastered this turbulent ocean, has 'fixed a limit which it must not pass' (148:6), has said: 'Thus far and no further' (Job 38:11); and if God relaxed his vigilance and ceased to exert his creative power, it would break out once more and engulf the world. The solidity of our world is to some extent an illusion. (Existentialist writers like Sartre, in *Being and Non-Being*, have tried to convey this idea.) It does stand firm; but only because God has fixed the pillars which support it (75:4); and it is over the turbulent waters that he has fixed it (24:2). It is only by the grace of God that the world continues, a continuing grace; our existence is precariously poised over an abyss of nothingness.

In the physical (or metaphysical) order, non-God may be nothing; but in the moral order there is something which is opposed to God, and that is evil. And the bible does not make such a clear distinction as we do between the physical and the moral. The waters of chaos, therefore, stand not only for non-being which God continually withstands by his creative power, but also for the power of evil which is always threatening to engulf God's good creation. The flood, of course, is the most obvious example of this; but a less wholesale and more personal calamity falling on the psalmist is described as 'the waters of death, the waters of evil' (18:5 f). The anguish from which he prays to be delivered is like 'the great waters' (32:6). The tragedy which strikes him is like the destruction of the world, when 'the mountains topple into the sea, when their waters boil and roar' (46:3 f; cf 42:8; 66:12; 69:2, 15; 124:4; 130:1).

Among the evils abhorred by the psalmist, enmity holds a prominent place. These enemies are sometimes described as beasts: 'many bulls encompass me, strong bulls of Bashan surround me; they open wide their mouths at me, like lions roaring and ravening . . .' (22: 12, 13, 16). There are of course many reasons why this type of metaphor should be chosen; but it is at least possible that it contains also an echo of the myth in which the enemies of God—the forces of evil—are presented as animals. This is even more probable in 91:13, where the man who is under God's protection 'will tread on the lion and adder, spurn with his foot the lion and serpent' (the same word being used here as the word for 'dragon' in the texts of Is 27:1 and 51:9 referred to above).

Creation is the victory of God; it is an act of the divine will, establishing his supreme dominion. And God's will is good. Evil—any evil: sin, sorrow, pain, the malice of enemies—is opposed to God's will. It is not only a pity, a shame, something to be deplored; it is an undoing of the divine plan, it is an insurrection of the primordial enemies of God, it is disruptive of creation.

The heavenly beings

In the myth, Tiamat's allies—'viper, dragon, sphinx, lion, dog, centaur'—are fixed in the heavens as constellations after their defeat in battle. This may have left its mark in the psalms in the references to the heavenly bodies as 'an army': the sun comes forth from his tent like a young warrior (19:6); 'by his word the heavens were made, by his breath all their army' (33:6); 'bless

Yahweh all his angels, mighty warriors who do his will'
(103:20).

But this last text leads us into a rather curious field of
thought, too far-reaching to be dealt with fully here.
Briefly, it is the question of the very ambivalent attitude
of the bible to heavenly beings; it is in fact a double ambiguity; in the first place, Israel, while quite clear that
Yahweh was the only true God, was never quite sure how
to think of the 'false gods' worshipped by other nations;
and secondly, if these false gods had any reality, were
they Yahweh's servants or his enemies? The influence of
mythological thought helps us to understand these ambiguities.

Belief in astrology was common in the ancient world,
and in fact underlies the myth we are dealing with; the
stars and other heavenly bodies are not inanimate ob-
jects, but gods, heavenly powers who have some influence
on human life and destiny. The boldest expression of this
in the bible is found in Deut 4:19: 'Beware of lifting up
your eyes to heaven, to the sun and moon and stars, all
the host of heaven, lest you be led astray to worship and
serve them, which your God has allotted to all the peoples
under heaven'—as if it were by God's express disposition
that the heavenly bodies were gods for people other than
Israel.

But Israel too sometimes recognises the gods as 'divine
beings' of some kind or other; as *elohim*, which is sometimes translated as 'angels' and sometimes as 'sons of
God': 'the morning stars sang together and all the sons
of God clapped their hands for joy' (Job 38:7). They
have, according to the myth, been vanquished by God
and reduced to subjection, and now form his court, his
servants: 'Bring to Yahweh, sons of God, bring to Yahweh glory and power' (29:1); 'Who is equal to God

among the sons of God—God, fearsome in the council of the holy ones, great and terrible among his court' (89:7 f).

But though defeated and subjected, they still have some power. We see this most clearly in the figure of the 'satan', the tempter, in the book of Job; he is one of the sons of God, a member of the heavenly court, but clearly not a joyful worshipper—he is an unwilling vassal who 'goes round about, roaming the earth', working what harm he can (Job 1:6–11). We see it too in the book of Daniel where divine beings are responsible for different nations and take their part in rivalry, 'the angel of the Persians' against the 'angel of Israel' (Dan 10:4–20).

Such divine beings are in fact particularly associated with human government, and civil authorities are themselves called *elohim*. They stand in the place of these angels and, like them, are not always completely reliable. They can thwart—or try to thwart—the divinely ordained right order as the star-gods allies of chaos did, and like them, they will be subject to divine judgement: 'Do you indeed, you *elohim*, proclaim justice? Do you judge the sons of men by just law? No, your hearts plot falsehood . . . O God, break the teeth in their mouths, break the jaws of these lions, that men may say, Yes, there is a God who judges all the earth' (58:1–12). 'God stands up in the divine council, in the midst of the gods he judges: How long will you make unjust judgements? . . . They walk in darkness; all the foundations of the earth are shaken. I said, You are gods, sons of the Most High; but you shall die like men, like other princes you shall fall' (82:1–8). Human judges and divine beings—they are so closely associated in the psalmist's mind that it is difficult to distinguish between them; the one plays out on earth the rebellion of the other in heaven, and both together, in their flouting of the divine will, threaten the order of creation.

What theological attitudes are expressed in this very mythological language? Ultimately, of course, this line of thought leads to the idea of 'good and bad angels' and 'guardian angels'. But more fundamentally, we are really here dealing with a concept which is basic to the whole bible, old testament and new: the concept of the kingdom of God. God's will is not completely worked out, not finished in a single act of creating ('My Father works until now, and I work', Jn 5:17). His rule, his kingdom, has to be established in all of creation. Christ himself is engaged in this work of 'subjecting everything to his Father' (1 Cor 15:27); and we too are involved in it, involved therefore in a struggle 'with the spiritual powers of evil in the heavens' (Eph 6:12).

In this struggle, however, God's providence still rules; nothing can harm us; 'no angel or prince or any power can come between us and the love of God' (Rom 8:38). Everything is at our service (1 Cor 3:23); indeed 'he has given his angels charge over you, that you may trample on the lion and viper, and spurn under foot the lion and the dragon' (91:11 f).

More fundamentally still, the bible is really expressing the uniqueness of God. It is not really interested in heavenly beings or heavenly bodies or the reality or otherwise of false gods. All that it is really interested in is summed up in the cry, 'Who is like to God!'

Who in the skies can be compared to God,
Who among the heavenly beings is like the Lord,
A God fearsome in the council of the holy ones,
Great and terrible among all that are around him?
Lord God of hosts, who is mighty as thou art? (89:
    6–8).

Creation and covenant

You cleaved the sea by your power,
You broke the heads of the monsters of the deep;
You crushed the heads of Leviathan
And made him the food of the wild beasts (74:13–14).

That these verses contain a reference to the creation myth scarcely needs to be argued in view of our earlier discussion; and it is made all the more evident by the clear reference to the creation in the verses which follow: 'You formed the light and the sun, you set the boundaries of the earth'.

And yet, apart from these verses, the psalm as a whole is dealing not with creation, but with Israel—Israel in distress recalls God's ancient mercies as the basis of an appeal for help now: 'You, my God, are my king from the beginning; you have brought us salvation.' In such a context, the reference to 'cleaving the sea' must inevitably call to mind the exodus. The conclusion is clear: the crossing of the Red Sea and the victory of God in creation have merged together.

We find the same in a psalm which we have already quoted several times for its references to the creation myth: 'The heavens proclaim your wonders, Lord; who in the clouds is like the Lord, who is equal to God among the sons of God? You mastered the pride of ocean; when its waves rise up you make them still. You cleaved Rahab like a corpse, and scattered your foes by the might of your arm. The heavens are yours and also the earth; the world and all that is in it you made, north and south you created' (89:6–13). Here again, the language and the immediate context point to the creation myth; but equally clearly the general context of the whole psalm— God's mercies to Israel—and the reference to the dividing of the waters would direct attention to the exodus.

The first article of Israel's creed was not: 'I believe in God, maker of heaven and earth', but: 'I believe in God who brought us out of the land of Egypt'. The exodus always stands first in Israel's mind, and it is in the light of this first, basic, revelation that everything else is understood. The waters, in the psalms just quoted, may indeed be the waters of chaos; but they are also the waters of the Red Sea. Rahab is the name for some mythical being; but it is also the name for Egypt.

But this has important consequences for our understanding of both the exodus and the creation. The exodus is a new creation. At the exodus, God was renewing and repeating, with special reference to Israel, his primeval victory. The God who made everything has chosen Israel, and the God of Israel is also creator of the world. We praise the glory of God in the heavens; but it is not some anonymous deity who thus reveals himself—it is our God whose glory is there: 'O Lord our God, how great is thy name in all the earth' (8:1). (Sometimes indeed there is a veiled polemic in these references to Israel's God in creation; as there is in the discrete insistence of Genesis that the heavenly bodies simply exist to give light—they are not in any way divine (Gen 1:14); or as there is in psalm 29:2 ff, where the 'sons of God' are summoned to transfer their allegiance to Yahweh, for it is he who is lord of all creation, it is his voice, not that of Baal Hadad, which is heard in the thunder.)

But more important still is the implication that creation, in a sense, is 'for' Israel. This is the point of the mingling of the two motifs in those psalms 74 and 89, an appeal to God the creator in the context of an appeal to the God of the covenant—because if the covenant should

fail, then creation itself would have failed: 'God has rejected us—the earth totters' (60:3 f). The 'faithful love'
which God has displayed in his choice and salvation of
Israel are the same qualities which keep the world in
being (89:3). Justice, love, truth—these are the qualities
of the God of the exodus and the God of Sinai; but they
are the qualities to be seen also in his creation (33:5;
36:6; 119:64). This is why the two parts of psalm 19 can
be sung together without any feeling of abrupt transition
—the law which God has given to Israel is his revelation
in the same way as creation itself. This is the thought in
the mind of the priestly author of the Pentateuch whose
series of linking genealogies connects Israel with the
patriarchs and then beyond them, with creation itself:
'These are the generations of heaven and earth ... of
Adam ... of Noah ... of Abraham' (Gen 2:4; 5:1;
10:1; 11:27). This is probably also in the mind of the
editor of the book of psalms in putting together psalm
104, dealing with creation, 105 dealing with the exodus,
and 106 dealing with the exodus and the entry into
Canaan. Certainly this is seen in Ps 136 which begins the
story of God's 'eternal love' with the creation and continues without a break into the signs of that same love in
Israel's history. There is a direct line of connexion between the creation and Israel; all creation is for God's
glory, 'his glory fills heaven and earth—and he has made
glorious his people' (148:14).

It is rather like St Paul's thought when he says to the
Corinthians: 'Everything, the whole world, is yours ...
and you are Christ's, and Christ is God's' (1 Cor 3:22 f).
It is very much the thought of the captivity epistles,
which view the mystery of salvation in the perspective of
creation: 'Christ is the first-born of all creation; everything was created in him, in heaven or on earth; every-

thing stands in him . . . And he is the head of the body, the church . . . It was God's good pleasure that the whole fulness should dwell in him and through him be harmonised, everything in heaven or on earth' (Col 1:15–20). So Israel stands at the heart of God's plan in creating; only through Israel will creation achieve its destiny, and if Israel should fail, then creation would have failed:

> Yahweh who provides the sun for light by day
> The moon and stars for light by night,
> Who stirs the sea, making its waves roar,
> He whose name is Yahweh Sabaoth says this:
> Were this established order ever to pass away
> Only then would the race of Israel cease to exist
>   (Jer 31:35).

This means that we must add another dimension to our reading of the exodus and the themes connected with it. The warlike language, for example, which is natural in the context of the great victory of the exodus, will now be seen to contain also an echo of the other great battle, of God against the forces of chaos; it is not merely Egypt which is defeated and the Red Sea which is quelled, but all the army of evil; and just as in later crises Israel appeals to the God who saved them from Egypt, so beyond that they appeal to the God who brought order out of chaos in the beginning, who brought life from non-being; and the enemies of Israel in any age form one with that army which opposed God from the beginning. This is particularly true of the great eschatological victory of God:

> The Lord is king! Let all the world rejoice
> A fire goes before him, devouring his rivals,
> His lightning lights up the world,

The earth sees and trembles, the mountains melt
like wax,
Before the master of all the world (97: 1–5).

The description is reminiscent of the exodus and Sinai;
but it is even more reminiscent of the victory of creation.
Creation, exodus and eschatological victory are all to be
seen in the same perspective. For the exodus was not
merely the redemption of Israel—just as the work of
Christ was not merely the salvation of souls; it involves
also the redemption of the whole of creation; it is the
beginning and the pledge of God's final perfection of his
creation: 'The whole of creation groans, awaiting the
redemption of the body' (Rom 8:22 f).

Finally, this association between the theme of creation
and the theme of the exodus gives us a further insight
into the psalmist's attitude to creation—the attitude we
are asked to adopt in using these psalms. The account of
creation has, so to speak, been brought into the history
of salvation. But the history of salvation is God's self-
revelation, to which we respond with faith and adoration. History is not merely the recording of past events,
Israel's history in the bible is not merely an epic; it is a
credo, and the recital of it is an act of faith. And the
psalms which praise God the creator (for example Pss 8,
19:1–6, 104) now partake of the same character. From a
purely literary point of view they have their parallels in
any other literature; but within the context of the bible
they are God's revelation of himself as the history of Israel was. As a poet, the psalmist may be moved by the
beauty of nature; as an Israelite, it is the glory of God
that he sees there, as he would see it in the temple. These
psalms are not an apologetic, arguing from the beauty of
creation to the goodness of God; still less are they an
aesthetic exercise, praise of beauty for beauty's sake;

they are a blessing, a *berakah*—a reaction of love and adoration to the God who reveals himself here:

> Praise him, sun and moon,
> Praise him, shining stars,
> Praise him, highest heavens.
> Let all earth praise Yahweh,
> Mountains and hills, orchards and forests—
> *Benedicite omnia opera Domini Domino* (148).

Ps 29

The loving appreciation of nature in Pss 104 and 148 is quite modern-sounding in its detailed observation; but it is always nature seen as a revelation of God's beauty, his power and his loving care. The continuity between the themes of creation and salvation in 74:12–17 and 89:9–12 has already been dealt with above; and the same can be seen in 147:8 f; 8 and 19:1–6 (cf pp 35 f).

Psalm 29 expresses in a slightly different way many of the ideas considered above. The poet's emotion as he contemplates the storm merges with his feeling of awe towards God. This fusion of contrasting emotions is completely typical of the bible, of the psalms in particular—the feeling of awe and almost of fear which is at the same time a feeling of delight and exultation; for it is 'our' God who is involved, the God who is 'for us'. We may indeed be moved with dread, to the very depths of our being; but it is not a mindless terror before a nameless power or blind fate. It is the feeling of Peter who says, 'Depart from me, Lord, for I am a sinful man'; or when he falls on his face before the transfigured Lord, but cries out, 'It is good for us to be here'.

There is some reason to think that the poem was based on a Canaanite hymn to Baal-Hadad, the god of the

storm; but it has been so thoroughly absorbed by traditional Israelite theology that it is hardly even polemic:
'It is the voice of Yahweh, not that of Baal-Hadad, which
is heard in the thunder'.

The glory of God in the storm is seen against the background of the heavenly court where 'the sons of God' do
homage to this majestic God, just as they 'shouted for
joy' to see the marvels of creation (Job 38:7); like the
seraphim who cry 'Holy, holy, holy' to the God whose
glory fills the whole earth (Is 6:3). For the origin of the
idea of 'sons of God', see p 32.

Contrasting with the order of the heavenly court is the
tumult of the storm (3 ff). The repeated 'voice of the
Lord' reproduces the sound of the thunder (the onomato-
poeia is even more striking in the Hebrew, *Qol Yahweh*),
rolling over the sea, bringing down the great cedars of
Lebanon, shaking even the mountains (the playful
image of the mountain skipping like a calf (6) strength-
ens the impression of power).

But this is not just the personification of nature by a
poetic imagination; behind the phenomena of nature
there is God, a personal God, one who has a voice, one
who spoke to Israel. It is the same God who appeared to
Israel in the wilderness of Kadesh and spoke to them in
the thunder at Mount Sinai (8). And so our response to
the power of the storm, in a single great shout echoing
the sound of the thunder, is 'Glory' (9).

'The Lord sits enthroned on the flood' (11); this is a
reference to the Hebrew picture of the world, with
waters above the sky, above which in turn God sits enthroned (Gen 1:7, and p 26 above). But it also contains a reference to the great 'battle of creation' in which
God mastered the unruly waters (cf pp 28 f). So the
tumult of the storm brings to mind the continual danger

from the forces of chaos, continually threatening to bring
the world to ruin again. Continually threatening, but
continually mastered; God's victorious liberation of Israel was a reaffirmation of his first, original, victory over
the waters of chaos in creation; and the temple in Jerusalem is a reminder and a guarantee of his continued
victorious presence. 'The gates of hell will not prevail.'

*Our view of 'creation' is inevitably more sophisticated than
that of the psalmists; indeed, we are more likely to speak of the
'environment' than of 'creation'. To what extent can we still
hold the psalmists' theological views as set out in the different
sections of this chapter? They probably thought almost mytho-
logically of the thunder as 'the voice of God'; can a thunder
storm speak to us of God's glory?*

4

The Lord's anointed

Need for kingship

The king holds an important place in the old testament, so important that a surprising number of psalms are devoted to him (2, 18, 20, 21, 45, 72, 89, 101, 132) as well as a number of references in other psalms. In order to understand this we have to look at the development of the monarchy in history. (This is another illustration of 'history as revelation'; the role of the king was not worked out in a priori theory or theology, but emerged from the apparently accidental historical circumstances.)

From Sinai, through the desert, and in the struggle for a foothold in Canaan, the social organisation of the people of God was tribal; it was a federation of tribes bound together by their covenant with God (it is sometimes called an amphictyony, on the analogy of the sacred league of the Greek city-states). This was not a particularly effective form of organisation; the tribal union was subject to conflicting strains, the claims of the individual tribes against those of the group. And in Canaan it was subject to still greater strains, as the federation absorbed new elements strange to its ways, and the tribes found themselves dispersed and scattered throughout the land.

43

Moreover, in addition to the practical difficulties of united action, the tribes were in fact deeply suspicious of any more centralised organisation. This was not merely because of their jealous feeling for independence; but because of their very status as 'the people of God'. It was not the accident of history or birth, or political convention that made them a people, but their covenant with God. The ties that bound them to Yahweh were the only ties that bound them together. There could be no other Lord over Israel, no other source of prosperity and success, no other source of law. They did of course have 'judges'; but these were 'charismatic' leaders, whose authority depended not on any official position or rank, was theirs not by right, but simply by the free choice and designation of God; it was moreover an authority limited to a specific occasion, and once that particular need had ceased so also did their authority. The principle of divine supremacy was thus safeguarded; they had no other king but Yahweh and nothing but his covenant held them together.

Eventually however they were forced to give some thought to a more effective form of organisation. The decisive factor was the danger from the Philistines—newcomers to Canaan, well armed and organised, who threatened Israel's precarious foothold in the land and even burnt Shiloh, the seat of the ark of the covenant (78:60).

It was then that many Israelites thought that the time had come to have a king 'like other nations', to rally the total military resources of the combined tribes. Others reacted strongly, on the grounds that we have just considered, that this was incompatible with their status as the people of God. It was indeed a dilemma: if they did not have a king, their national existence was threatened, they would cease to exist as a people; if they did have a king, they would cease to be what they were, the people of God.

The practical needs of the situation won the argument, and they elected Saul as king. They solved, or shelved, their dilemma by regarding him as a charismatic leader like the judges. But the position of a permanent charismatic was too difficult to sustain, and Saul eventually took his own life in a last disastrous battle with the Philistines. The position was then as before, with an experiment in monarchy that had failed, and the Philistines still undefeated. It was then that David appeared on the scene.

David's position was quite different from that of Saul. He had been driven into exile by Saul's jealousy and, living as an outlaw, he built up a force of skilled and seasoned troops. With these at his back when he returned home after the death of Saul, it would have been a brave soul who would have asked awkward questions about charismatic leadership. And yet it is impossible to dismiss David as a military dictator, a soldier of fortune canonised because of his success. He was deeply conscious of the position of Israel as the people of God, and he had no wish to usurp the position of God as leader of the people, nor to ride rough-shod over the sacred traditions of the covenant.

One act of his above all symbolises this: as soon as he had captured Jerusalem and made it his capital, he transferred there the ark of the covenant. We will have occasion later to deal more fully with the significance of the ark, but the importance of this move is quite clear; his capital is also the covenant shrine; the subjects of the king are still subjects of the covenant; the ideals of the covenant were not to be discarded and ignored, but were safe in his hands.

The covenant king

But to say that the covenant and the monarchy were identified would have been ambiguous. In any state at that time it could be said that politics and religion were not clearly distinguished; but this could mean that the state was the servant of the god, or that the god was the servant of the state. Which was it to be with David? We are back to the original dilemma; and in order to bring out quite clearly the course chosen by David, let us make clear the possible solutions. First, they might have clung to the covenant and rejected the idea of monarchy—a solution they had decided was impractical. Secondly, they could have opted for monarchy and discarded the covenant—a solution they found unthinkable. Or thirdly, it would have been possible to think of having both covenant and kingship, but separating their roles—the king being supreme in political matters, while the covenant principle continued to be accepted in non-political affairs. It was the third solution that David was excluding by enshrining the ark in his capital. What he was saying was that the monarchy does not replace the covenant, but that somehow or other the two are combined.

Somehow or other; but fortunately there were already analogies in contemporary thought which suggested a solution. There was especially the idea of corporate personality which was strongly rooted in Israel's thinking; the idea that a person does not exist simply as an isolated individual but as a member of the group to which he belongs; so that the whole group, family or tribe, could be regarded as realised in a person who represents them. This would be true of the founder of a family, and it would be true of the king. Israel's king contains the whole people of Israel. If they are bound in a covenant with

Yahweh, this covenant is concentrated, so to speak, in the person of the king; he is the embodiment of the covenant.

Or again, it was customary in some civilisations at that time to regard the king as the adopted son of god. In Canaanite legend the king is called 'son of El, offspring of the kindly one, a holy being'. But Israel too was son of God by virtue of the covenant (cf p 17). The language of Canaanite kingship could then be applied to Israel's king in his role as embodiment of the covenant people: 'He will call me "my father", and I shall make him my first-born' (89:26 f); 'You are my son, today I have become your father' (2:7).

All that is true of the covenant, then, is now true of the king: 'I have made a covenant with my chosen one, I have given my servant David my oath' (89:3). The king is a sacred person; and in token of this he was anointed. This anointing—pouring out the richness and strength and joy of oil on the king—became part of the coronation ceremony, and the king was known as 'the anointed one', the messiah.

But with the use of this term, a new train of thought opens up; it was a term and an idea which was to have a fruitful history. The monarchy was not just an accident of history, and David himself was more than just a skilful politician who happened also to have a remarkable insight into the religious demands of the nation. Through him, that theology itself was enriched, and the monarchy became a central feature of Israelite religion.

For the covenant idea won acceptance not only for David but also for his descendants, for his dynasty. This is expressed in the oracle of 2 Sam 7:5–16, when David was planning to build a temple for Yahweh: 'You will not build me a house; I shall build you a house . . . Your

house and your sovereignty will always stand secure before me, and your throne be established for ever'. The
covenant with the nation, resting as it did on the faithfulness of God himself, was a bond which continued from
age to age. But the covenant, linked with the established
order of creation (cf pp 37 f) was now focussed on the
dynasty: 'I will keep my love for him always, my covenant with him shall stand. I have founded his dynasty to
last for ever, his throne to be as lasting as the heavens. I
will not break my covenant, I will not revoke my oath.
His dynasty will last for ever. I see his throne like the
sun, enduring for ever like the moon' (89:28–37).

Each successive king, then, was hailed as 'the messiah'.
But successive kings failed to live up to the ideals they
set for him, failed to bring about the hopes they reposed
in him. Israel did not then abandon their hopes and
ideals. Disillusioned with the kings they had, they looked
even more fervently to a king of the future. Their hopes
did not fade, but became deeper and more insistent; and
the psalms which expressed this hope were projected onto
the ideal messiah to come.

The messiah

The covenant stood for unity above all else; and unity is
above all what David brought to the people. We have
seen that the picture of a single united Israel following
Moses out of Egypt, marching in unison through the
desert and invading Canaan as a single force, is largely
the projection of a later age. In reality, it was the separation of the tribes which was much more marked. Moreover, as the tribes came together gradually, some of them
formed links more easily and quickly than others, and in
this process there was a tendency to coalesce into two

groups, a northern and a southern. David realised that this dual polarisation was in a way more dangerous than the fragmentation of the twelve tribes, and from the beginning he was at pains to heal this division. He himself belonged to the southern tribe of Judah and was quickly accepted by them and set up his headquarters at the southern town of Hebron. Saul's followers were mainly from the north and resented the idea of this newcomer taking Saul's place. David did all he could to conciliate them. He executed the man who claimed to have helped Saul to suicide, showed respect for Saul's dead body, and restrained his men from retaliating when they were provoked by Saul's adherents. This policy eventually won over Saul's followers, and it was then that David moved to Jerusalem. This in fact was a major factor in his choice of that city as his capital. It was not the most important town in the land, its capture cost him some difficulty; but it had the great advantage that it was a 'new' city—it had been in Canaanite hands until then, it had no associations with any group who could claim it as 'their' city, it was fairly central geographically, unlike Hebron in the south or Shechem in the north. In making Jerusalem his capital and transferring there the ark of the covenant, he was proclaiming his dedication to the ideal of unity which the covenant demanded and which the ark symbolised. It was on this more than any other single fact that the glory of David in Israelite tradition rests: that the covenant established an ideal of unity, and David made it a reality.

This unity was in fact short-lived. The folly of David's successors reawakened the latent jealousy between the northern tribes of Israel and the southern tribe of Judah, and the north finally broke away: 'To your tents, Israel; what have we to do with the house of David' (1 Kg

12:16). This began a split which was in fact to cripple
the nation for the rest of its history. But the ideal of union
still remained, and it was hoped that the messiah, the
ideal king descended from David, would restore the work
of his father. The prophet Ezekiel, in a typical symbolic
gesture, took two pieces of stick, one inscribed 'Israel',
the other 'Judah', and joined the two together: 'I shall
make one stick out of two, one king is to be king of them
all; they will no longer be two nations nor form two
separate kingdoms. My servant David will reign over
them, one shepherd for all' (Ez 37:15–24). The messiah
stands above all for unity, 'he has broken down the
separation between us and made the two into one, unit-
ing them in a single body' (Eph 2:14).

But David did more than unite the tribes; he united
also the whole country; Jerusalem was more than a tribal
centre—it was a real national capital. Canaan was
occupied by different peoples of different races without
any unifying authority. But now the whole country,
Israelite and non-Israelite, was united under David's
rule. The battles for occupation had been bloody; by the
only rules of warfare known at that time land was gained
by the slaughter of the inhabitants. But after the capture
of Jerusalem, there is no report of wholesale massacre,
neither in Jerusalem itself nor in any of the other
Canaanite cities, and yet there is no sign of any further
resistance. Even the Philistines are only heard of after
this as members of David's bodyguard. We can only presume, but we have every right to presume, that all the
heterogeneous peoples who made up the population of
Canaan found a new unity under the rule of David. They
presumably accepted David's God also—this would be
normal practice for the time. This would not involve any
deep religious conversion and would be the seed for

trouble later. But for the moment David had brought unity to the country.

And after the Canaanites, it was the turn of other peoples round about; Aramites, Edomites, Moabites all accepted David's leadership in one form or another, and Egyptians to the south and Phoenicians to the north were brought into alliance through marriage (the marriage with the princess of Tyre is celebrated in psalm 45). And so Israel's vision goes out to a world-wide empire united under their one king: 'Blessed be his name for ever, enduring as long as the sun! May every race in the world be blessed in him and all the nations call him blessed' (72:17)—the echo of the promise to Abraham is evident (Gen 12:3). 'His empire shall stretch from sea to sea, from the river to the ends of the earth; the kings of Tarshish and of the islands will pay him tribute, the kings of Sheba and Seba will offer gifts, all kings do him homage, all nations become his servants' (72:8–11). 'You place me at the head of nations, a people I did not know are now my servants, foreigners come wooing my favour' (18:43 f). It is a vision which is continued in the last book of the bible, when 'people from every nation, race, tribe and language shouted aloud: Victory to our God and to the Lamb' (Rev 7:9).

But if the king is victorious it is not by his own strength: 'Yahweh save the king. Some boast of chariots, some of horses, but we boast in the name of Yahweh our God' (20:7–9). Like the covenant people whom he represents, he relies on Yahweh's help, his wars are God's wars, his enemies God's enemies, God's faithful love is with him. 'His king he saves and saves again, displays his love for his anointed, for David and his heirs for ever' (18:43–50). 'You are my son, today I have become your father. Ask and I will give you the nations for your heritage, the ends of the earth for your domain'; if he is son, he is heir also. 'My hand will always be with him, he will be able to rely on my arm; no enemy will be able to outwit him, I myself will crush his opponents. I will give him control of the sea, dominion over the rivers. With my faithfulness and my love his fortunes will rise in my name'—faithfulness and love, *hesed we'emeth*, the covenant qualities.

The king's victories are even described in language reminiscent of the phenomena of Mount Sinai, and like this, this language in turn has overtones of God's cosmic victory (cf pp 38 f). 'The earth quivered and quaked, the foundations of the mountains trembled, from his nostrils a smoke ascended and from his mouth a fire that consumed. He bent the heavens and came down. Yahweh thundered from heaven, the Most High let his voice be heard; he let his arrows fly. The bed of the seas was revealed, the foundations of the earth were laid bare' (18:7–15). His enemies too are described in terms that recall the creation myth: 'The beast will cower before him and his enemies grovel in the dust' (72:9); 'The waves of death encircle me, the torrents of evil burst over me, the snares of death were before me' (18:4 f).

The king is the source of prosperity for the nation. One might say that this is the role of any government at any time; but in some of the magical ideas attached to kingship at that time, it was regarded as the special prerogative of the king through his special association with the gods. So an Assyrian king says: 'From the time that the gods placed me on the throne, Adad made his rain fall, Ea opened her springs, the corn grew five cubits high, the harvest of the land was abundant'. But in Israel, these blessings were the blessings of the covenant: 'Listen to these ordinances, be true to them, and Yahweh will be true to the covenant. He will bless the fruit of your body and the produce of your soil, your corn, your wine, your oil. No man or woman among you will be barren, no male or female of your beasts infertile' (Deut 7:12–15).

But these are not just natural hopes for a comfortable and successful life. The account of the fall at the beginning of Genesis expresses this; the afflictions which beset human existence—social, natural and moral disorder, suffering and death—are not congenital and are not intended to be permanent. Somehow, sometime, humanity—'the offspring of the woman'—will rise above them. These hopes are then projected onto the messianic king. 'Listen now, house of David: the maiden is with child and will give birth to a son whom she will call Immanuel. On curds and honey will he feed until he knows how to refuse evil and choose good. On that day, where once a thousand vines grew, all will be thorn and brier' (Is 7:14–24). On the face of it, this is an assurance that even if the present king should fail, even if the land were reduced to a wilderness, the dynasty will not fail; there will be a successor embodying God's promise to be 'with' his people, 'Immanuel'. But in addition there are echoes of the text of Genesis in the phrases 'to refuse evil and choose good', and 'thorns and briers'. This is even clearer in another passage in the same prophet; a king will come in whose days 'the lion will lie down with the lamb, the panther lie down with the kid, calf and lion-cub feed together with a little child to lead them . . .' (Is 11:1–9).

What the Israelites expected from their ideal king, then, was not merely good government nor magical prosperity, but paradisal peace, the repair of our fallen state: 'Yahweh, the king rejoices in your saving power. You have granted him his heart's desire, you have met him with the choicest blessings. He asked for life, and you gave it to him, length of days for ever and ever' (21:1–4). 'Lord, give your blessings to the king; let the mountains and hills bring a message of peace for the people; grain everywhere in the country, even on the mountain tops, abundant as Lebanon its harvest, luxuriant as common grass' (72:1.3, 16).

But if 'the serpent's head' is to be crushed (Gen 3:15), it is not simply prosperity which has to be assured, not only national enemies which have to be overcome, but the evil in men's hearts. Israel's prosperity in fact was always connected with morality; her prosperity was a covenant blessing and was attached to the will of God expressed in the covenant law: 'If you live according to my law I will give you the rain you need, the earth shall give its produce . . .' (Lev 26:3). And the king too could rely on Yahweh's help if he lived by Yahweh's will: 'Yahweh requites me as I act justly; as my hands are pure so he repays me. His judgements are all before me, his statutes I have not put away from me' (18:20–24). The king is lawgiver; but the law he imposes is not his personal will, but God's law; he is in fact the keeper of the nation's conscience: 'I will not let my eyes rest on any misconduct. I hate the works of those who fall away. He who walks in the way of the blameless shall minister to me. No man who practises deceit shall dwell in my house. I will destroy all the wicked in the land' (101:3–8). Justice is a quality of any good government, but from Israel's ideal king it was God's justice that was expected: 'Lord, give your own justice to the king, your own righteousness to the king's son' (72:1); 'Your royal sceptre is a sceptre of equity; you love righteousness and hate wickedness' (45:7). Under this just rule, the country is rich in more than wealth and crops: 'In his days may righteousness flourish, the mountains and hills bear prosperity' (72:7, 3). Moreover, it is not a cold, legal justice that is expected from the king; like God's justice it is also *hesed*, loving mercy, going out most to those in need: 'Give your justice to the king so that he may rule your poor with justice. He delivered the needy when he calls, and those who need help. He will redeem their lives from oppression and violence, their blood will be precious in his sight' (72:1, 2, 12–14).

It was not, therefore, a purely formal equivalence that was made between the role of the king and that of the covenant people; he enters into the very heart of the covenant relationship. This is seen again in the sacred character attributed to the king. Israel was a holy people, a consecrated nation, a kingdom of priests (Ex 19:6). The king did not displace the traditional priesthood vested in the descendants of Aaron, but he was 'a priest according to the order of Melchisedech' (110:4). Melchisedech was an ancient king of Jerusalem who entered into an association with Abraham (Gen 14:18–20); in accordance with a fairly common custom, he combined the office of king with that of priest. The reference to him in the psalm, as prototype of David's king-priesthood, may have been intended to win the favour of the Canaanite occupants of Jerusalem, by presenting David as his legitimate successor. But it was also appropriate to the covenant ideology that the leader of the people as a state should also represent them in worship; that he who was expected to bring prosperity to the nation should also offer the fruits of that prosperity in worship.

The covenant means unity: not only harmony between men, but union between men and God; the covenant means that 'God is with us'. The king represents this aspect of the covenant too; he stands very close indeed to the divine, and the vision of the ideal king expresses this in terms which come very close to apotheosis. Of course it was impossible for Israel's determinedly monotheistic faith to attribute divinity to a human being. But we have seen how they came to regard him as 'son of God'. He was 'Immanuel', God with us. His kingdom was spoken of in terms of God's kingdom: 'Ask and I will give you the nations for your heritage, the ends of the earth for your domain' (2:7); 'His empire shall stretch from sea to sea, from the river to the ends of the earth' (72:8). His throne is at God's right hand (110:1), and his royalty has more than human origin (110:3). He exercises God's own role as 'shepherd'; 'I have taken him from following the sheep and made him shepherd of my people Israel' (78:70). This is a reference to the tradition that David had been a shepherd in his youth; and shepherd is a conventional metaphor for king; but is used in a much more than conventional sense of Yahweh, 'the shepherd of Israel, who leads Joseph like a flock' (80:1). A song for a royal marriage merits a place in Israel's hymns (Ps 45), and those who sang this hymn in the liturgy could not fail to think of God who had espoused Israel in the covenant. The same poem even refers to the king as a divine being: 'Your throne, God, will last for ever' (45:6). It is true that the word here translated as 'God', *El*, is used also of other beings than the deity himself. But it is difficult to see what more could be added—until God's only Son became our king, became Immanuel; overcame all God's enemies including the last enemy, death, and established God's kingdom, a kingdom of light and life in which we achieve unity with each other and union with God.

Ps 2

Psalm 18 is mainly a 'lament', a prayer of thanksgiving for deliverance (and therefore most of the relevant ideas belong to a later section, pp 83 f). It is only towards the end (18:43–50) that it becomes apparent that it is concerned with God's mercies to the king specifically. Attempts to split the psalm into separate parts have not been successful; it is merely that the king was so important in Israel's thought that his experience of deliverance was important to every Israelite. So also Pss 20, 21, and 89:19–37—the covenant with the nation and the covenant with David almost overlap. The same idea is expressed in a slightly different way in 61:6 and 63:11; these are not royal psalms, but the psalmist found it natural to include a prayer for the king in his own prayer, for God's mercy to the king was a guarantee of his mercy to the psalmist. Similarly in 132 God's presence in the temple is interwoven with the thought of his presence in their king. The royal wedding song, 45, has a place in the psalter because his wedding is a 'sacrament' of the betrothal of God and Israel. The ideas in 72 have been largely dealt with above. We will deal here with 2 (with which 110 has much in common).

'Why do the nations conspire?' In the ancient world the accession of a new king was regularly an occasion for unrest; subject peoples and their rulers thought this might be an opportunity to cast off their bonds and re-gain their independence. So the enthronement of a new king in Israel was also an occasion for asserting his con-tinued authority. Israel was never actually in such a position of world-wide dominion, with subject kings fretting under her yoke. The language is simply adopted from the conventional court language of great powers like Egypt or Assyria. But the psalmist realises that what is involved in the enthronement of Israel's king is not his personal power or the nation's glorification, but the kingdom of God.

The thoroughly militaristic language, then—'Let us burst their bonds . . . You shall break them with a rod of iron' (2:3, 9)—is in a familiar tradition. It is the language of the exodus: 'The enemy said: I will draw my sword, I will divide the spoil . . . Thou didst stretch out thy hand, the earth swallowed them, horse and rider thou didst cast into the sea' (Ex 15:9, 12). And this in turn echoes the language of the creation myth, where God 'breaks the head of the dragon of the waters' (74:13). The king's enemies are not human foes, but the enemies of God, 'the rulers of this world, the powers of darkness, the spirits of wickedness on high' (Eph 6:12).

And it is indeed an 'uprising', this challenge to God's supremacy: 'I will ascend to heaven, above the stars of God, I will set my throne on high' (Is 14:13). It is an act of futility and folly. It is not by brutal domination, by invasion or by savage military repression that God rules. His rule is our freedom; in his will is our peace.

But the high and holy God has come down to us, has put himself within our reach—accessible to our attack if we would have it so, or pledge of his love as he intended. The temple is the sign of his presence with his people; and enthroned on Zion too is the anointed king, sign of God's peace-bringing rule. Other kings were called 'sons of god'; but for Israel's king it is more than a formula of protocol. He is the embodiment of the covenant people, called to such a closeness of relationship with God that they are indeed God's sons. The covenant with the nation was focussed on the king specifically. The proclamation of the enthronement was at the same time a proclamation of God's covenant with him. He was the bearer of a divine will which transcended the historical reality. His claim to universal dominion is not the pathetic pretension of a petty middle eastern ruler, any more than Jesus was deluded when he made the astonishing claim: 'All authority is given to me in heaven and on earth'.

The king is the bearer of God's rule, therefore any attack on his rule would be an attack on God. And although such opposition could be described from one point of view as folly, something which leaves untouched the reality of the divine dominion; nevertheless, from another point of view it does provoke God's anger: he speaks in wrath and terrifies them in his fury (2:5), his wrath is quickly kindled (2:11), the king will break his enemies with a rod of iron (2:9). (It was a common practice to inscribe an enemy's name on a pot, which was then broken, thus magically bringing about the destruction of the enemy.) But this does not express irritation or outraged pride. It is an expression of God's absolute and unqualified rejection of all that is evil. His will is our good; but it is also a demand that we take our freedom seriously: 'Serve the Lord with fear . . . Blessed are all who take refuge in him'.

1. What meaning does kingship, as seen in these psalms, retain for us?

2. How do the 'messianic' psalms apply to our Lord? cf Ac 2:36f; 13:30–33; Eph 1:19–23; Col 1:15–20.

3. In what sense does 'God's kingdom', and 'the kingship of Christ' imply domination?

5

The place where the glory dwells

The temple

Urban civilisation is a very dubious concept today; but in principle at least we still recognise that 'civilisation' is connected with the city. It is the expression of man's social instinct; men group together, and by their combined efforts master their environment and develop their resources in wealth, art and culture.

This concept has a place in biblical thought too. The ideal state of man is described as a garden, an oasis in the barren waste; the harsh reality is described as expulsion from the garden into a wilderness of thorns and briers. The desert is an unwelcome, eerie place, 'where jackals have their lair and ostriches nest, where wild cats and hyenas prowl, vipers brood and kites gather; where satyrs call to one another and the night hag alights and finds her resting place' (Is 34:12–15).

It was out of this 'howling wilderness' that God led Israel, into the land flowing with milk and honey. There they settled in cities and David built them a capital, the city of Jerusalem. The strongly-walled city was their protection against enemy attack and protection against the unwelcome desert; it gave them a feeling of security and confidence, of having reached a home after the years of danger and wandering. It signified at least a partial fulfilment of the covenant, when 'each man lived secure, under his own vine and his own fig-tree' (1 Kg 4:25).

Of Jerusalem itself, then, they spoke with pride and joy: 'Number her towers, see her ramparts, go through her citadels, that you may tell the next generation' (48:12). But to appreciate fully the tone of passionate enthusiasm with which they spoke of it, we must go deeper than patriotism, even religious patriotism.

Israel's God was holy, 'other'—not merely frightening or awe-inspiring or mysterious, but really different from us and from anything that lies within normal human experience (cf p 13). He is 'out of this world'. We belong to this earth; in normal, 'pre space-age' language, we speak of 'the heavens' as being what lies beyond our world. So, 'heaven is the Lord's; earth he has given to the sons of men' (115:16). He is even above that; he has to stoop to see the sky and the earth (113:6). 'As high as the heavens are above the earth, so are my ways above your ways and my thoughts above your thoughts' (Is 55:8).

The bible pictures the original state of man as one of intimacy with this holy God, he 'walked with them in the cool of the evening'. But sin cut them off from God; the peaceful security of his presence was replaced by terror, and familiarity by separation.

God did not then desert them or abandon them entirely. He still cared for them, still protected them, and still showed disapproval for their sins. But the word now used is that he 'visits' them; a misfortune could be 'a visitation' from God, or he might 'visit' them with blessing.

And whenever God visits men, wherever the holy God manifests his presence, there was a 'holy place', a place to be regarded with terror and awe. A typical example is found in the story of Jacob: Jacob dreams of a ladder pitched between heaven and earth, on which angels go up and come down—a sign of God's continual protection for him; and when he woke up, Jacob said: Truly, the Lord was in this place; it is a place of terror, it is the house of God, it is the gate of heaven. And he poured oil over a stone and set it up as a monument; and this is given as the origin of the holy place of Bethel (which can be translated 'house of God').

Since God is the source of life, his presence was particularly associated with springs which make the earth fruitful, or with trees. So too are mountains and hills, whose heights bring man closer to the heavens where God is. The bible often refers to idolatrous worship 'on every high hill'; and in Canaanite legend the gods assemble on Mount Saphon, 'the mountain of the north' (rather like Olympus in Greek legend).

A 'high place' might be artificially constructed; at a place where worship was to be carried out or a shrine was to be set up, a mound of some kind might be erected to symbolise the idea of the god 'dwelling on high'. The best example of this is the Mesopotamian 'ziggurat'—a stepped tower with a shrine at the top and another in the base, representing the god's dwelling on high and his coming down to earth (Jacob's ladder mentioned above obviously refers to this; it is 'the house of God and the gate of heaven').

To denote the idea of 'otherness', the whole area round a holy place was cut off from profane contact; as when Moses approached the burning bush and was told: 'Come no nearer; the ground on which you walk is holy ground' (Ex 3:5). The same happened at Mount Sinai; when the people arrived at this mountain where God was to manifest himself, Moses was instructed: 'Mark out the limits of the mountain and tell the people: Take care not to go up on the mountain or to touch the foot of it. Whoever touches the mountain will be put to death' (Ex 19:12).

It is against this background that we think once more about the covenant. A holy place was one where God manifested himself to men; but in the covenant God not only visited his people but joined himself to them; he was 'Immanuel', God with us. His presence with them was symbolised by the ark; not a fixed site but a holy place that would go with them on their journeys, housed in a tent as they themselves lived in tents. And when the people adopted a settled form of life and lived in cities and houses instead of tents, the presence of God with them was signified by a permanent building. This was the temple.

At Sinai, God had inaugurated a new stage in his relationship with men, and now that relationship has been made permanent. What happened at Sinai was now transferred to the temple on Mount Zion: 'The Lord has come from Sinai to this sanctuary' (68:17). 'He has pitched his tent on Zion' (72:2) as once it was pitched amongst Israel in the desert. Just as there Moses saw him face to face, so now all Israel come to the temple 'to see his face' (42:2; 27:8). This is the true 'mountain of the north', home of the gods according to the Canaanites: 'Mount Zion, in the far north, city of the great King' (48:2); 'Why look you with envy, O many-peaked mountain, at the mount which God desired for his abode' (68:16). God's 'place' is heaven; but when the ark is transferred to the temple, God makes this his palace: 'Arise, O Lord, and go to thy resting place, thou and the ark of thy might. The Lord has chosen Zion, he has desired it for his habitation: This is my resting place for

ever, here I will dwell' (132:8, 13 f). The heavenly phenomena which betoken the presence of the God of heaven
are now associated with the temple: cloud covered Sinai
when God came down there, and a cloud filled the temple
when it was consecrated (1 Kg 8:10). 'He built his
sanctuary like the high heavens' (78:69). The Lord's
throne is in heaven, and it is also in the temple (11:4).
The cherubs which stand by the ark represent the
heavenly beings which accompany God's heavenly
chariot: 'He bowed the heavens and came down, he rode
on a cherub and flew, he came swiftly on the wings of the
wind' (18:9 f).

This sort of language made it very easy for the ordinary
Israelite to think of the temple as the place where God
actually lived, as the pagans thought of their temples as
houses for the gods. Orthodox theology of course was
always clear on the fact that God could not actually
'live' in any building: 'Heaven and the heavens cannot
contain you; how much less this house that I have built'
(1 Kg 8:27); 'Heaven is my throne and earth my foot-
stool; what house could you build for me' (Is 66:1). But
this was not so clear in popular thought. This was particularly true when the temple became the only place of
worship for Israel. In the early days of their occupation
of Canaan, they took over many of the Canaanite holy
places; and though the shrine of the ark was always the
central national sanctuary, worship was also carried out
at these other holy places. But idolatrous customs crept
in at these other shrines, so eventually it was decided to
abolish them, leaving Jerusalem and the temple the only
legitimate place. But this only increased the danger of
regarding it as the place where God had his home. We
can see this when Israel was exiled; even a fervent
Israelite felt that he was cut off from God when he was

cut off from the temple: 'By the waters of Babylon we sat and wept, when we remembered Zion ... How can we sing the Lord's song in a foreign land' (137:1, 4).

But it was then that the prophets triumphantly proclaimed God's power which is not restricted to any little parcel of earth: 'Am I a God when close at hand, and not a God afar off? Do I not fill heaven and earth?' (Jer 23:23 f). The danger of localising God in the temple was an opportunity to make clear again what the temple really was. It was not a house in which God lived; it was a symbol—a sacrament, even—of the only real presence of God, which is in his people. God is not present 'in'; he is present 'to' or 'with'; and it is in virtue of the covenant that he is present with his people. The temple is nothing more—and nothing less—than a visible sign of this bond between God and man.

What then is involved in this bond which the temple signifies? It is in the first place a demand, summed up in the law (with which we shall deal again later). We have already seen that the covenant could be visualised as a treaty, and it is in accordance with this analogy that the terms of the treaty were laid up in the ark. But in the ark there was nothing else, no statue or image of their God; the law *was* the expression of God to them, and in their following of the law they came close to God. One of the prophets, protesting against the superstition of regarding the temple as a house for God, expresses this forcibly: 'Do not trust in these deceptive words: This is the temple of the Lord, the temple of the Lord, the temple of the Lord' (with this parrot cry the people reassured each other when the city was in danger, as if the temple were a talisman): 'Will you steal, murder, commit adultery, swear falsely, and then come before me? But amend your ways and your doings, and then I will dwell in this place' (Jer 7:4–11, 3).

The temple is a holy place, not by any magical *mana* which clings to it, but because it is a sign of the holiness that God expects of his people. But this gives a new dimension to the concept of holiness. In an earlier stage, holiness meant terror of the God who was 'other'; to approach him, or anything consecrated by his presence, was dangerous: 'Take care not to approach this mountain, or you shall die' (Ex 19:12); when the ark was being transported to Jerusalem the man who in an excess of zeal put out his hand to steady it was struck dead (2 Sam 6:6). To fit oneself to approach God involved ritual purification as a magical precaution: washing, wearing new clothing, fasting, and abstinence from sexual intercourse. But gradually, holiness came to take on a moral connotation, with a clearer awareness of the moral quality of their God: 'Be ye holy, because the Lord your God is holy'. This is the significance of psalm 15 (cf 24:3–6): 'Who may come to the holy mountain?' This sounds like a ritual challenge to those preparing to enter the temple, and might have been expected to be followed by a warning like that given to the people at Mount Sinai or to David when he sought to use the sacred bread as food (1 Sam 21:14): 'Who may come to this holy place? Only those who have washed, only those who have abstained from intercourse . . .' It is in striking contrast to this, then, that the psalm puts forward moral qualifications: 'Who may come here? The man who does what is right, who speaks truth from the heart, who does not slander, who does not take bribes.'

The covenant law was enshrined in the ark; and therefore God, the lawgiver, was regarded as enthroned on the ark. We have already seen how the thought and language of God's 'heavenly' dwelling was applied to the temple (cf p 63). The thought of God their leader in battle was also applied to the ark: 'As the ark set out, Moses would say: Arise, O Lord and let thy enemies be scattered' (Num 10:35); and when the ark was installed in the temple, God's victorious power was exercised from there: 'Mount Zion, city of the great king; within her citadels, God has shown himself a sure defence. For lo, the kings assembled, they came on together. As soon as they saw it, they were astounded, they were in panic, they took to flight' (48:3–5); 'His abode has been established in Salem, his dwelling place in Zion. There he broke the flashing arrows, the shield, the sword and the weapons of war. At thy rebuke, O God of Jacob, both rider and horse lay stunned. But thou, terrible art thou! Who can stand before thee? From the heavens thou dost utter judgement; the earth feared and was still, when God arose to establish judgement, who cuts off the spirit of princes, who is terrible to the kings of the earth' (76:2–12). Here, as so often in Israel's battle-hymns (cf pp 29 and 35) there are suggestions of God's warfare with more than simply human foes: 'God is in the midst of the city, she shall not be moved. The nations rage, the kingdoms totter; he utters his voice, the earth melts. Therefore, we will not fear though the earth should change, though the mountains shake in the midst of the sea, though its waters roar and foam, though the mountains tremble with its tumult' (46:5 f, 2 f); 'The floods lift up their roaring; mightier than the thunder of many waters the Lord on high is mighty—holiness befits thy house' (93:3–5).

The covenant promised not only victory, but peace; and the temple is a sign of this peace: 'God is in the midst

of the city; he makes war cease to the end of the earth;
he breaks the bow and shatters the spear' (46:5, 9).
'Those who trust in the Lord are like Mount Zion. As the
mountains are round about Jerusalem, so the Lord is
round about his people' (125:1 f). This image of God
encircling his people like the city protected by the surrounding hills recalls the other image of the outspread
wings of the cherubim in the temple: 'Let me dwell in
thy tent for ever. O to be safe under the shelter of thy
wings' (61:4); 'I have looked upon thee in thy sanctuary, and in the shadow of thy wings I sing for joy'
(63:2, 7). The name 'Salem', sometimes used as a
shorter form of the name Jerusalem, suggests the Hebrew
word for peace, *shalom*; and some texts seem to refer to
this connexion: 'Pray for the peace of Jerusalem; peace
be within your walls, and security within your towers'
(122:6 f).

But *shalom* does not mean merely peace in the sense of
cessation of hostility. The root meaning is 'completeness',
and peace in the bible signifies the prosperity and richness of life which is the expression of God's presence with
his people. The temple in Jerusalem is a sign of this
shalom. 'The children of men take refuge in the shadow
of your wings. They feast on the abundance of thy house,
and thou givest them drink from the river of thy delights.
For with thee is the fountain of life; in thy light do we see
light' (36:7–10). The 'waters of death', the waters of
chaos (18:4, cf p 30) are not only subdued but
turned into the waters of life: 'We will not fear though
the waters roar and foam. There is a river whose streams
made glad the city of God, the holy habitation of the
Most High' (46:2–4). It is like a new garden of Eden,
from which four great rivers flow (Gen 2:10); and
Ezekiel sees a rich, life-giving stream coming from the

right side of the temple, flowing down through the barren desert of Judah and even sweetening the waters of the Dead Sea (Ez 47: 1–12). A pilgrim psalm pictures the earth breaking out in fruitfulness as the pilgrims make their way to the temple: 'As they go through the valley of Baca they make it a place of springs, the early rain also covers it with pools' (86:6).   *7. Joy*

So the temple is the symbol of the joy they expect from the presence of God: 'Let my tongue cleave to the roof of my mouth if I do not set Jerusalem above my highest joy' (137:6); 'As a hart longs for flowing streams, so longs my soul for thee, O God. My soul thirsts for God, for the living God: when shall I come and behold the face of God?' (42:1 f). 'How lovely is thy dwelling place, O Lord of hosts! My soul longs, yea faints, for the courts of the Lord' (84:1 f). 'I was glad when they said to me, Let us go to the house of the Lord' (122:1); 'When the Lord restored the fortunes of Zion we were like those who dream. Then our mouth was filled with laughter, and our tongue with shouts of joy' (126:1).   *8 Unity*

But the most striking mark of the covenant was unity —unity between the tribes, presaging unity between all men. It was when David transferred the ark to Jerusalem that this unity began to be accomplished, and the temple remained the sign of it. This is made manifest in the city itself, binding men together in harmony and security inside its walls: 'Jerusalem, built as a city which is bound firmly together, to which the tribes go up, the tribes of the Lord' (122:3 f). And like David's kingdom, it becomes a centre for all nations: 'God reigns over the nations, God sits on his holy throne. The princes of the people gather as the people of the God of Abraham' (47:8 f); so that eventually Jerusalem will be the spiritual home and focal point of unity between all

nations of earth: 'Glorious things are spoken of you, city
of God. Among those who know me are Rahab and
Babylon, Philistia and Tyre and Ethiopia: "This one
was born there", they say. And of Zion it will be said,
"This one and that one were born in her". The Lord
records as he registers the peoples, "This one was born
there"' (87:3–6).

The sign of the temple was fulfilled when the word became flesh and 'tented' in our midst (Jn 1:14). He is the
reality of God's presence with us, the ladder pitched between earth and heaven (Jn 1:51). There is now no need
for a temple; it will be destroyed, and will be replaced by
the temple which is his body (Jn 2:19–21). This will be
the focus of worship, not the temple in Jerusalem nor any
other (Jn 4:21). Out of his side shall come living water
(Jn 19:34; 7:38; 4:14), which will unite men to him in
the Spirit; so that they too will form one temple with
him, 'living stones joined to the living stone making a
spiritual house' (1 Pet 2:4 f), where the Spirit of God
dwells (1 Cor 3:16). So that here we achieve our union—
'no more strangers or foreigners, but part of a building
which has Christ Jesus as the cornerstone, growing into
one holy temple in the Lord' (Eph 2:19–21).

Ps 48

Jerusalem and the temple are signs of God's protection
of his people and the prosperity he promises (46, 65,
76:1–3; 132). It is the focal point of the national unity
(122) and even of unity for all men (87). To approach
the holy God dwelling there, moral qualities are necessary (15, 24). Ps 137 expresses the love and longing of an
exiled Israelite for the temple. Ps 48 centres on it.

48:1–3. Jerusalem was an ancient city, capital of the nation, a stronghold, a centre of wealth and culture. But it was also the 'sacrament' of God's presence with his people. It was not in its strong walls, but in God that Israel found defence. It was not its architectural beauty and magnificence that evoked their pride and admiration; but the fact that it was a symbol of the beauty of God's own heavenly dwelling.

The pagans pictured their gods dwelling somewhere 'in the far north'—safely inaccessible. But our God is both further away and nearer. No place on earth can contain him; but he has united himself with his people—but for all mankind (v 2, joy of all the earth).

48:4–7. May refer to a specific event like the invasion of Sennacherib from which the city was miraculously delivered (2 Kg 18–19). But in any case behind this stands God's continual saving, protecting power; as in Ps 2, the assembled kings are neither historical nor simply eschatological, but any and all human power confronting the majesty of God. This confrontation is real, even if invisible; God's power is not normally seen in its visible nakedness; but for those who do perceive it—for the psalmist and for us—the reaction is dread and exultation.

48:8–11. It is not an attitude of gloating over a defeated enemy, but delight in the power of God. The victory over enemies is just one way of expressing his power to save: 'Fear not—I have overcome the world'; 'Rejoice not that the spirits are cast down from heaven, but rejoice that your names are written there' (cf Lk 10:18–20). And this saving power is always present; it is not limited to a single specific occasion, it is experienced by the worshippers now: 'As we have heard, so have we seen . . .' The very city in which they are assembled is the pledge of God's steadfast love. The temple is not merely the place in which they happen to be to remember his mighty love; it is itself the sign of that loving presence.

48:12–14. In some more superstitious ideas, God's holiness was like an aura, an emanation, which could strike dead one who approached incautiously, but which could also imbue a worshipper with the very power of God. A pilgrim to a holy place, then, could go home and hand on this power to those who had not been so privileged. But here it is not any magical power that the pilgrim takes away with him; it is renewed faith, and this awareness of the love and power of God is handed on not only to fellow-citizens at home, but to future generations and to all mankind.

'He spoke of the temple of his body' (Jn 2 : 21); 'You are like living stones united to him, the corner-stone, to make a living temple' (1 Pet 2 : 5). For a christian, the church is the only place where God dwells. How does this concept add to our understanding of the psalms, and what do the psalms add to our understanding of the church?

6

A light to my feet

Torah

In an age which so values the freedom of the individual, it is difficult to be really enthusiastic about authority—even when it is the authority of law. We may accept it, we may recognise its necessity or value; but it is difficult to imagine being moved to sing about it. This is not less true in religion—it is even especially true here, since religion claims to foster the growth of the human spirit, appeals for a free response from the heart. A response which is patterned on the dead letter of a law comes uncomfortably close to phariseeism.

Yet in the psalms the law is presented as a subject for prayer, for devout pondering, for lyric rejoicing. If we are to make such prayers our own, we have to see what lies behind the psalmist's attitude.

At the very beginning, we come up against the problem of language, the question of translation. The word which is generally translated as 'law' is in Hebrew *torah* which might be more literally translated 'instruction'. This instruction is found in many different forms and in many different contexts in the bible; but one would expect to find it most obviously in the didactic books of the bible.

The instruction given here is good advice—the lessons

of age handed down by a sage to his disciples, by a father to his son: 'Hear, my son, your father's instruction . . . forsake not your mother's teaching'. Most of it is rather prosaic and practical: 'Wine is a mocker, strong drink a brawler; the dread wrath of a king is like the growling of a lion; it is an honour to a man to keep aloof from strife; the sluggard does not plough in the autumn' (Prov 20:1–3). It reminds one of the homilies of old Polonius to his son: 'Neither a borrower nor a lender be.' Its purpose is to teach *savoir-faire*, how to make a success of life: 'So you will find favour and good repute in the sight of God and man' (Prov 3:4). Of course, this could never be divorced from God, and one sage finds all he has to say, the height of wisdom, summed up in the law: 'All of this is the book of the covenant of the Most High God, the law which Moses commanded. It fills men with wisdom, fills them with understanding' (Sir 24:23 f). And at the end of it all, the wisdom we seek, the wisdom to which this instruction guides us, is the wisdom of God himself: 'Breath of the power of God, a pure emanation of the glory of the Almighty, a reflection of the eternal light, a spotless mirror of the working of God, an image of his goodness' (Wis 7:25 f). When the psalmist speaks of 'the law', this is the sort of thing he would have in mind.

He would have in mind too the teaching of the prophets, for this too is called *torah*, instructions: 'Bind up the testimony, seal the teaching among my disciples' (Is 8:16). And there was no one more anti-legalistic than the prophets. Much of their teaching was devoted to a condemnation of legalism, the formality of ritual practices divorced from the service of the heart: 'This people honours me with their lips, but their hearts are far from me' (Is 29:13). Their denunciations and their passionate appeals for service from the heart—this is included in the concept of *torah*, instruction.

But the word *torah* is used especially for what we would call the Pentateuch—the first five books of the bible, the five 'books of Moses'. And it is reflection on this that breaks the bonds of narrow legalism that the English word 'law' always seems to threaten. For although the Pentateuch does contain a great deal of legal matter, it also contains very much more. It begins with the account of man's sin and God's promise of redemption; it is the story of Abraham's call, his following in faith, and God's promise to him of a son through whom all men would be blessed; it is above all the account of God's great act of redemption which is the exodus and the formation of a people who are wedded to him in a covenant. All of this is *torah*.

Finally, however, we must not evade the fact that *torah* is also used for what in any language we would call 'law'; that in the long didactic poem on the law, Ps 119, it mentions 'precepts', 'statutes', 'ordinances' and 'commandments'; that the Pentateuch is probably called *torah* because it does contain legal codes—the precise rubrics for sacrifice, the penal rules concerning restitution and damages, detailed distinction between clean and unclean animals, scrupulous concern with legal purity.

According to the literary convention which probably determines the form of the covenant, these laws were the 'terms' of the treaty (cf p 16). These are the wishes of the Lord, binding on the loyalty of his subjects, the conditions on which they were assured of his favour. But the covenant also formed the basis of Israel's national existence—it brought them into being as a people (cf p 17); and if we look at it from this point of view, then the law is their constitution; the people of God has the law of God as its foundation.

But the law of God is not arbitrary whim, designed merely to extract our obedience. It is, according to one of the many synonyms used in Ps 119, his 'word'; through it, God enters into communication with man, he reveals himself. God reveals himself in various ways—through the events of history, through the world in which we live, through prophets; and he reveals himself also in his laws. But this tells us how we are to regard these laws; we are to regard them as revelations of God, just as much as the creation, the story of Abraham or the account of the exodus. In all of these God is communicating with us, and he is communicating with us also in his commandments.

We have seen that the word *torah*, which is often translated 'law', could better be translated as 'instruction'. But the root of the word means 'to cast'—a reference to the practice of casting lots to decide a course of action. There was a time when men had to rely on such practices to discover the will of God—omens, auspices, oracles. The custom was recognised in Israel's religion too; the *Urim* and *Thummim* (Ex 28:30; Num 27:21) were a form of 'lots' by which primitive guidance was given. It probably consisted of two stones in a pouch, one designated positive and the other negative, so that whichever was picked out of the bag represented God's answer; David consulted this after Saul's death, and received the answer that he should return to Judah and that he should go to Hebron (2 Sam 2:1). But to have the guidance of God by law, instead of such non-rational means, was an immense advance. It was a sign of Israel's coming of age. God now spoke to them as men, in the full light of reason, rather than as beings just emerging from the half-light of instinct and superstition. The prophets remind Israel how unfitting it was that reasonable men should use any other means of learning the will of the living God: 'They say to you, Consult the mediums and the wizards who chirp and mutter. Should not a people consult their God? Should they consult the dead on behalf of the living? Look rather to the teaching!' (Is 8:19 f).

The law is, according to another of Ps 119's synonyms, 'witness'; it gives testimony, it tells us what sort of a God he is. It is the expression of his nature, his character. It is in fact simply because the law is an expression of God's nature that they are rules for us, his children, called to be like him. This revelation of God is at the same time a revelation for man, of what he is called to be. Morality is connected with the word *mores*, which means a characteristic manner of action; our morality is not on the one hand blind instinct nor on the other hand mechanical observance of the letter of a law, but a way of acting based on the character of God himself.

'All the paths of the Lord are steadfast love and faithfulness.' The way of the Lord is in the first place the route of the exodus (cf p 20); it was there that they learned to know him, to know that he is faithful love. But the law is the concrete expression of his way, his 'rod and his staff' (23:4) guiding us to life.

Therefore although Israel's religion is certainly a religion of law, it is far from being legalist. The law is a grace, a light, a privilege: 'What other nation is so great as to have statutes and ordinances so righteous?' (Deut 4:8). Other nations had idols and images to represent their god to them; Israel had the law. Other nations sought his guidance in omens and oracles; Israel heard his voice in the law. The threat of legalism always hangs over a religion which accepts a code of law; but this is a form of idolatry at least as pernicious as the idolatry it was meant to replace. This was never the meaning of law in Israel. It was a means by which we may model our actions on the way of acting of God himself, mould our way of thinking to his, our hearts to his: 'I call heaven and earth to witness against you this day, that I have set before you life and death; chose life, that you may live, loving the Lord your God, obeying his voice and cleaving to him, for that means life to you' (Deut 30:19 f): 'You shall love the Lord your God with your whole heart and with all your soul and with all your might. And these words shall be upon your heart; you shall talk of them when you sit in your house, when you walk by the way, when you lie down and when you rise' (Deut 6:5–7).

The ideal, then, is that the time shall come when we shall not need a written code of rules to guide us, but our minds and hearts shall be so full of the spirit of God that this alone shall be our law: 'the days are coming, says the Lord, when I will make a new covenant with the house of Israel . . . I will put my law within them, and I will write it on their hearts' (Jer 31:31–33).

The psalms in praise of the 'law', then, are very much more than hymns to a code of laws. We have in mind, when we pray these psalms, above all the idea of God's revelation of himself. This revelation does have practical implications, implications for our daily living, and these are expressed in specific precepts; but the precepts are to be seen as revelations of God's will for us and of his own nature.

And finally, all that is meant by *torah* is found in Christ. He is the word, in whom God reveals himself fully. The *torah* is the story of God's promise of salvation:

and all God's promises reach their goal in him (2 Cor 1:20). The *torah* is found in the instruction of the sages; but he is our wisdom (1 Cor 1:24). He is the way, the truth and the light (Jn 14:6). And if we needed (and still need) guiding rules, it was as a 'pedagogue' to lead us to Christ (Gal 3:24). He now not only shows us how to live but has given us the power to know and to do (Phil 2:13); united with him we live by his Spirit and carry his law in our hearts.

For us as for the psalmist law is not a burden grudgingly accepted; it is something we long for and pray for, our pride, our delight, our guide, our life.

Ps 1

Not many psalms (1, 19, 119) deal with the law explicitly, though there are frequent references to it, to which the above section will apply. Here we will see how these ideas apply to Ps 1 (which was probably put as an introduction to the whole psalter by an editor who saw in the law the summing-up of all God's revelation).

'Blessed is the man . . .' This is a familiar formula in the didactic literature of the bible—as it is in all didactic literature; it is the assurance of one who claims to have the answer to man's questioning and questing: 'You seek for happiness? This is where it is to be found'.

Or rather, first, where it is not to be found. For many conflicting answers are given to this question, many different directions are given; and the psalmist describes first the process of going astray (*walks, stands, sits*). There are people who pay no attention to the prohibitions and taboos and sanctions of religion, and they seem to do very well out of it, apparently untroubled by pangs of conscience or remorse: 'They are not in trouble as other

men are, they are not stricken like other men . . . Therefore the people turn and praise them; these are the
wicked, always at ease, they increase in riches. All in
vain I have kept my heart clean' (73:5, 10, 12, 13). This
surely is the answer; this is the way. So a man may follow
it, hesitatingly at first and occasionally troubled in
conscience. But gradually the doubts fade and he settles
confidently into it. And in the freedom of this broad
road he can look with contempt on the narrowness of
those who are held back by petty inhibitions and the
cowardice of conscience.

But these are the trite commonplaces of moralists; and
as with any other moralist, the psalmist prejudges the
issue by the use of pejorative terms: 'wicked, sinners,
scoffers'. But the issue *is* prejudged. This is what revelation means. God has shown us the way to live; he has not
left us to the ambiguity of instinct or the uncertainty of
logic. Not that he gives clear-cut answers to specific
questions either. Revelation means in the first place not
answers from God but that God has come to be with us.
God's 'way' is for Israel the road which led from Egypt
out into the desert, from slavery to freedom, from death
to life. This was the road which God himself first
walked, and along it he led his peoples like a shepherd.
Only in following this way was there safety; stray
from this, and a man is lost in the pathless, waterless
waste.

All this experience Israel summed up in the law. Law
is not an arbitrary display of authority. It is the expression of truth (like a law of nature—and indeed it is a law
of nature, of God's nature and ours). It is not a peremp-
tory dictate to be obeyed mindlessly. It is a revelation of
the kind of God we worship, and of the kind of person
we should be in following him. It is a light, a grace, to be

pondered and savoured. 'Blessed is the man who meditates on his law'.

Such a man is like a tree . . . This is a very natural figure of speech in a land like Palestine, where the absence of water means a bare and barren waste where only a few withered shrubs survive, and where an oasis or the spring rain means richness and fertility, with olive trees and vines growing firm-rooted and fruitful.

But it is also a figure with a long history. It was this image of a tree-planted garden which represented to Israel's man's original state of happiness with God; and the hope of restored happiness was expressed in the promise of a fertile land where God himself dwelt, 'like a cedar of Lebanon, like a palm tree in Engaddi, like the cyprus of Hermon, like the roses of Jericho, like the olive in the plain, like the plane tree by the waters' (Sir 24:13 f). And finally, Israel itself was like a tree—their deliverance from Egypt reproduced the miracle of growth from a barren land, the beauty and fruitfulness of God's protecting presence: 'Thou didst bring a vine out of Egypt' (80:8 ff). In one who follows the law, Israel's destiny can be fulfilled. Outside of this there is only fatuity; not only barrenness, not even the stunted growth of the desert scrub—less even than this; chaff, the useless husks that remain after the corn is removed.

This is our faith; a firm faith, resting on the truth of God, on God's own revelation of himself. But it is still faith, not evident experience. It is not free from the doubts that can assail us when faithfulness to God results only in poverty—not only material poverty, but the much worse poverty of spirit, the blight of our natural growth. But the tree brings forth its fruit only 'in due season'; before that it must be pruned so that it may bring forth more fruit. We must be purged, 'tested as gold is tested by fire, so that our faith may be shown worthy of praise and glory and honour' (1 Pet 1:7). These sufferings are the birth-pangs through which a new man is brought forth, one who is moulded to the likeness of God through conformity to the law in which God has revealed himself.

Only where this likeness to God exists is there life; outside of God there is nothing. 'The way of the wicked will perish'. There is the horror of the abyss in these words; not the abyss of a picture-book hell, but simply the abyss of nothingness. God does not need to punish these; though they flourish like the green bay tree, there is a cancer at the heart which eats through and leaves— simply nothing.

This too suggests an answer to the simple absoluteness of the psalm. Good-evil, saint-sinner, black-white; it is rather more absolute than most of us would like; at any given moment most of us could not be too sure which side we are on. But the simplicity and absoluteness are the expression of God's absoluteness. For us, it is a prayer; it is an act of faith, an act of hope, an act of charity; it is the expression of our allegiance to that ideal. To that extent we are taking sides with God; there is at least this much in us that God can 'know'. The rest, it is the task of our lives and God's purging to destroy.

1. What is the relationship between 'the law' and 'command-ments'?

2. 'Christ is the end of the law'; in the light of that, how do we pray a psalm like this?

7

Out of the depths

The goodness of God

The psalms are prayer. They are about God, but they are
also therefore about man. They contain lyrical, joyful
adoration and thanksgiving to God; but they speak from
the reality of the human situation, and so they deal also
with human hopes, human needs, human desires. To call
these 'psalms of petition' is not enough. Probably more
than half the psalter is indeed composed of cries for help
and laments in sorrow; but nearly all the psalms in one
way or another reflect Israel's hopes and ideals. So we
have not really come to grips with Israel's thoughts, we
cannot really make their prayer our own, until we have
considered their attitude to what is most fundamental in
human life—the question of good and evil.

Basic to Israelite thought is the confident optimism
expressed in the first page of the bible: 'God saw that it
was all very good'. All; and the bible thinks naturally of
the visible, tangible world around us. Man's ideal state
is described as life in a garden, untroubled by toil, pain
and death; and Israel's hopes continued to be expressed
in similar terms: hopes for a land flowing with milk and
honey, where each man lives under his own vine and his
own fig-tree (1 Kg 4:25). This ideal continued to elude
them, but they continued to hope for a day when 'the

83

wolf shall dwell with the lamb, and the leopard lie down
with the kid' (Is 11:6–9); when 'the mountains will drip
sweet wine, and the hills flow with milk' (Jl 4:18).

The concept of 'life' itself fits into the same thought-
pattern. Life does not mean mere existence; life is a share
in God's life—'God breathed into his nostrils the breath
of life, and he became a living being' (Gen 2:7); and any
life worthy of the name included happiness, prosperity,
success. Death of course was a fact of nature; man lived
on only in his children and in the community of which he
was part. The real tragedy and mystery of death was that
it involved separation from God, the source of all life and
source of all good. 'Death' means sickness, persecution,
shame, misfortune—all that makes life less worth-while:
'Thou hast delivered my soul from death, my eyes from
tears, my feet from stumbling (116:8).

We do not do justice to the thought of the psalmist if
we try to allegorise such statements, if we try to make
them metaphorical statements of some 'spiritual' ideal.
The thought is quite simple and straightforward: God is
good, so everything that comes from him must also be
good. This is not just an expression of a natural human
characteristic, of the hope that springs eternal in the
human breast. It is not arrived at by projecting into an
imaginary world the ideals so sadly lacking in the real
world. It is the result of a certain idea of God, not the
result of an idea of human life. God is perfect; therefore
his works must be perfect. The bible does not, and we
need not for the moment, consider the difficulties this
gives rise to (the obvious imperfections of the world); but
in any case we must not allow the difficulties to obscure
or compromise the basic idea, that God's goodness is expressed in creation.

God's goodness is expressed in creation: its goodness is

the expression of his goodness, its beauty the expression of his, the joy it gives is the joy of his giving. Therefore to love and desire good things—food and drink, beauty, prosperity, success—is to love and desire the goodness of God. We are familiar with such prayerful sentiments as 'praising the greatness of God', 'adoring his glory, 'thanking him for his goodness'. But how in fact can we know these qualities of God, how do we experience them, if not in the things he has done? 'O Lord, how majestic is thy name'—but the psalmist goes on: 'How majestic is thy name in all the earth, thou whose glory is in the heavens' (8:1). 'O Lord my God, thou art very great'; but it is in his works that we see it: in the wind which he rides like a chariot, in the mountains and valleys which he has formed, in the earth which is full of his creatures; he is 'clothed with honour and majesty—but it is in the glory of the sun that we see his majesty, he is 'clothed with light as with a garment' (104:1 ff).

Nor is this an objective, detached, disinterested emotion. We appreciate God's goodness even and especially when it is shown to us personally: 'Lord God, how great thou art', David prays: and this feeling is not prompted by any speculative considerations, but by God's promise that his dynasty would last for ever, 'thou has promised good things to thy servant' (2 Sam 7:18–28). 'Give thanks to the Lord, for he is good, for his steadfast love endures for ever'—to him who led Israel through the Red Sea, defeated our enemies, and gave us a land (136: 14, 17, 21). It is in these things that God has revealed himself, and if he has not revealed himself, how do we know him? If we have not experienced his goodness—if we have not known love, or joy, if for example we have not drunk wine that makes glad the heart of man (104: 15)—what does it mean when we praise his goodness?

To 'bless' God, means that we recognise his blessings to us.

This is true of the blessing of life itself: 'I shall not die, but I shall live and recount the deeds of the Lord' (118: 17). It is not merely that the time of life is to be occupied in praise, but life itself is a gift of God, and in the living of it we praise God: 'In death there is no remembrance of thee, in Sheol who can give thee praise? . . . I will extol thee, O Lord, who hast brought up my soul from Sheol; will the dust praise thee, will it tell of thy faithfulness? But thou hast turned my mourning into dancing, that my soul may praise thee' (6:5; 30:1–11).

Of course this means that life is only really good in so far as it is the expression of God, the living God, source of all good. Without him, the goods we seek are just illusion, 'vanity', shadows. But this is not a denial of the principle, it is just a further expression of it. Those whose 'portion in life is of this world' (17:14), those who rely on the riches they have acquired (52:7) instead of on the rock that is God, rely on something that has no substance. 'Better a little that the righteous has than the abundance of many wicked' (37:16). For God alone is the real blessing. The Israelite hopes for the land flowing with milk and honey; but 'the Lord is my portion and my cup' (16:5). God's love is better than life itself (63: 3); 'I have no good apart from thee' (16:2). Therefore, even if all our hopes and expectations should fail, it is no falsehood to look to God, the good behind all good: 'Whom have I in heaven but thee? And there is nothing upon earth that I desire but thee. God is the strength of my heart and my portion for ever' (73:25).

It is in this way in fact that the doctrine of the future life develops in Israel. Christian readers sometimes find it surprising that throughout most of the old testament—

in most of the psalms, for example—there was no awareness of a future life in our sense (the dead were thought to
continue some sort of existence in Sheol, in the under-
world, but it was only a shadowy half-life). Reasons for
this apparent blind spot need not concern us here; but it
does make it all the more admirable that old testament
devotion was not based on the sort of refined self-interest
which may lie behind our own more developed theology.
For the psalmist, life—not a life beyond the grave, but
life now—was the blessing of God and the happiness of
that possession. But God is a living God, whose existence
is not ended with our death: 'I know that my Redeemer
lives, and at last he will stand upon the earth, when my
skin has been destroyed' (Job 19:25 f). Even in Sheol he
is present (139:8), and even the dead must adore him:
'Before him shall bow all who go down to the dust' (22:
29). The delight of his presence is the delight of un-
limited life: 'The children of men take refuge in the
shadow of thy wings. They feast on the abundance of thy
house, and thou givest them drink from the river of thy
delights. For with thee is the fountain of life; in thy light
do we see light' (36:7–9). 'I am continually with thee,
thou dost hold my right hand' (73:23). 'Thou dost show
me the path of life; in thy presence there is fulness of joy,
in thy right hand are pleasures for evermore' (16:11). It
is in this way that the idea begins to dawn—a desire that
becomes a hope that becomes a conviction—that death
does not end our relationship with the living God: 'In
thy right hand are pleasures for evermore ... Therefore
my heart rejoices, my soul is glad, my body also dwells
secure. For thou dost not give me up to Sheol' (16:9 f).
Our Lord himself sums up the whole argument suc-
cinctly; in answer to an objection by those who even then
found the idea of life after death difficult to accept, he

merely draws attention to the traditional formula that God is 'the God of Abraham, the God of Isaac and the God of Jacob', and then points out the implication: 'He is not God of the dead, but of the living' (Mt 22:32).

A modern reader, then, can pray these psalms with no mental reservation but only with greater awareness of how much the life of God means to us: 'I believe that I shall see the goodness of the Lord in the land of the living' (27:13).

Perfect hate

The attitude that we have been exploring—the utter conviction of the psalmist that God is the God of good— explains another aspect of the old testament which is inclined to shock a new testament reader, the unabashed detestation of all forms of suffering. 'Happy shall he be who takes your little ones and dashes them against the rock' (137:9); this is rather difficult to make our own in prayer, when we also try to follow the Lord's injunction to give good for evil.

Once more, we do not for a moment pretend that such sentiments are the height of christian charity; but neither can we dismiss them as simply crude vengefulness, simply a vivid reminder of the imperfection which Christ came to bring to perfection, but without any real value for us. On the contrary, there is something here which may well be a valuable reminder for us too.

If God is the God of good, then evil is no part of his will; it is something to be deplored, disliked and even hated. If we really believe that God is good, we do him no credit if we accept placidly and complacently all that is wrong in our world. Whatever is wrong—sin, suffering, poverty, injustice, falsehood, calumny—is a failure of God's wishes; *all* of it is wrong, every aspect of it.

This explains a curious feature of the psalms of lamentation. There are a great number of these, and quite clearly they are the expression of a deep and real anguish; 'How long, O Lord? Wilt thou forget me for ever? How long must I bear pain in my soul?' (13:1); 'Hear a just cause, O Lord; give ear to my prayer from lips free of deceit! From thee let my vindication come!' (17:1); 'My God, my God, why hast thou forsaken me? O my God, I cry by day, but thou dost not answer; and by night, but find no rest' (22:1 f). Yet when we come to examine them more closely, it turns out to be surprisingly difficult to pinpoint exactly what is the specific source of distress. Take Ps 6, for example. 'Rebuke me not in thy anger' (6:1) might seem to imply a consciousness of guilt; and 6:6 also seems to imply a feeling of sorrow and mental anguish: 'I am weary with my moaning, every night I flood my bed with tears'. But it is not simply mental anguish; it is physical suffering too that he prays to be released from: 'Heal me, for my bones are troubled; save my life, for in death there is no remembrance of thee' (6:2–5). Yet a little later it appears that it is not only sin and God's punishment that are at stake, but somehow or other human enmity as well: 'My eye wastes away because of grief, it grows weak because of all my foes. Depart from me, all you workers of evil . . . All my enemies shall be ashamed' (6:7–10). We see much the same pattern in Ps 37: 'O Lord, rebuke me not in thy anger; thy arrows have sunk into me; there is no soundness in my flesh because of thy indignation, there is no health in my bones because of my sins . . . I am utterly spent and crushed, I groan because of the tumult of my heart' (37:1–10); and then again he prays for deliverance from his enemies: 'Those who are my foes without cause are mighty, and many those who hate me wrongfully, those who render me evil for good' (37:19 f).

Much might be said about these enemies. Certainly, the traditional association between sin and suffering (with which we shall have to deal later) is concerned here; the psalmist's suffering is hard enough to bear, but in addition this suffering is taken to be a sign that he is a sinner, so that in addition he has to bear the calumny of his acquaintances: 'There is no health in my bones because of my sin . . . My friends and companions stand aloof from my plague. I pray: "Only let them not rejoice over me"' (37:3, 11, 16). In other psalms again one may suspect a background of 'trial by ordeal' such as is referred to in Ex 22:7: 'If a man delivers to his neighbour money or goods to keep, and it is stolen out of the man's house, if the thief is not found, the owner of the house shall come near to God, to show whether or not he has put his hand to his neighbour's goods'. The psalmist, then, in response to his accusers, comes before God to protest his innocence and ask for justice: 'Vindicate me, O Lord, for I have walked in my integrity' (26:1); 'O Lord my God, save me from all my pursuers. If I have done this, if there is wrong in my hands, If I have requited my friend with evil or plundered my enemy without cause, let the enemy pursue me and overtake me, let him trample my life to the ground. Judge me, O Lord, according to my righteousness and according to the integrity that is in me. O let the evil of the wicked come to an end, but establish the righteous, thou who triest the minds and hearts, thou righteous God' (7:1–9; 'Hear a just cause, O Lord, from thee let my vindication come. If thou triest my heart, if thou visitest me by night, if thou testest me thou wilt find no wickedness in me, O saviour of those who seek refuge from their adversaries. They are like a lion eager to tear, as a young lion lying in ambush' (17:1–12).

But this last phrase may give us a clue; it leads us to similar phrases in the psalms which speak of these enemies in a revealing way: 'Be not far from me, for trouble is near and there is none to help. Many bulls encompass me, strong bulls of Bashan surround me; they open wide their mouths at me like a ravening and roaring lion. Yea, dogs are round about me. Deliver my soul from the sword, my life from the dog. Save me from the mouth of the lion, my afflicted soul from the horns of the wild oxen' (22:11–21). We have already met this figurative language in the 'creation myth' (cf p 28); and the use of it here puts this question of suffering onto a different plane. God's work in creating was visualised as a battle against the forces of evil, portrayed as animals. Now human enmity is portrayed with the same animal mask; and rightly. All that mars God's perfect order is opposed to God; and this human enmity, knowingly or unknowingly, is taking sides in this primordial warfare. Evil undoes the work of creation. A corrupt judge, for example, may seem to be a social scandal, serious indeed, but no more than that. But for the psalmist it is more radically destructive: 'How long will you judge unjustly? The foundations of the earth are shaken' (82:1, 5). When he suffers from enemies, from those who hate him without cause, it is the floods of primeval chaos that he feels sweeping over him. Oriental hyperbole, no doubt; but it is true that for those who believe in a good God and his good creation, no form of evil can be treated lightly. It was to just such human enemies, motivated by the quite normal human passions familiar to us—jealousy, avarice, callousness—that our Lord says: 'This is your hour, and the power of darkness' (Lk 22:53).

The life of man on earth is a warfare (Job 7:1); but our struggle is not merely with flesh and blood, but with the spirits of wickedness in the heavenly places (Eph 6:12). It is an element in the eschatological warfare mentioned so often in the bible (cf Rev 12); eschatological not in the sense that it will take place only at the end of time, but in the sense that on it the fate of the world depends. This too gives us further insight into those protestations of innocence: 'I was blameless before him, he recompensed me according to my righteousness' (18:23 f). We have already said something of the situation which gives rise to such expressions, but they still sound to us uncomfortably hypocritical. But they have a different ring when we put them into this context of warfare. In this warfare, we must take sides; and by the very fact of our prayer, to this extent at least we are taking the side of God.

And this is true even when we realise that in this warfare the enemy has a citadel within our own hearts. There is the first stronghold to be overcome, and it is on this evil in ourselves that we first turn our hatred and our loathing.

Death—and life

We have traced one aspect of the psalmists' thoughts on good and evil, and have tried to see what permanent values they embody, valid even for us today. But if this were the whole of their thought, it is difficult to see how the psalmists could ever have coped with the problem of suffering. And certainly they had a long and difficult struggle with this problem, in the course of which several different insights emerged, never completely synthesised and never forming a completely satisfactory solution (but have we arrived at one even today?).

We may begin again with the basic thesis, 'God saw that it was all very good'. The Israelites did not make our distinction between moral and material good and evil; for them all aspects of both good and evil formed a totality. Happiness, prosperity, good fortune went hand in hand with virtue and the presence of God; and the absence of good—misfortune, suffering, pain—was a sign of the absence of God, or what we would call sin. In fact the word sin can be used to describe such misfortunes. Leprosy, for example, is not merely an ailment calling for medical care, but a lack of divine blessing calling for purification, reparation and a 'sin-offering' (Lev 14:1–20). It would not be true to say that they were unaware of moral responsibility, but it is true that they were even more aware of a unified 'right order', of a total relationship between man and God affecting every aspect of our lives.

Suffering then is a sign of the absence of God. But it is only a short step to say that suffering is a *punishment* for sin; and this the story of the fall seems to express— though it would perhaps be more accurate to say that sin and suffering are connected rather as disease and symptom; if we separate ourselves from God, the absence of all other expressions of God's goodness follows as an inevitable consequence, as the outward sign of the real evil. It is an example of the working of the simplest law of justice, an eye for an eye and a tooth for a tooth: 'With the loyal thou dost show thyself loyal . . . and with the crooked thou dost show thyself perverse' (18:25 f).

But this simple operation of the law of retribution, this 'punishment', can easily be a means of bringing the sinner back to his senses, making him see the folly of his ways and turning him back to God. The clearest exposition of this is the 'theological thesis' of the book of Judges (2:11–19). The people entering Canaan fell into idolatry—they were punished by falling into the hands of their enemies —in their affliction they repented and prayed to God— who then sent them judges to free them from their enemies. 'Blessed is the man whom thou dost chasten, O Lord' (94:12); 'Happy is the man whom the Lord reproves; therefore despise not the chastening of the Almighty. For he wounds, but he binds up, he smites, but his hands heal' (Job 5:17 f).

This is what might be called the 'classical' theology of Israel: since God is the God of all good, the virtuous man will enjoy prosperity, the sinner will be deprived of good things, if a man is suffering in any way it must be because he is a sinner. The only trouble is that it does not fit the facts, it is not true to experience. It never was. Nevertheless, it could continue to be viable as long as Israel's view of corporate personality continued to be accepted—a man's sufferings could be due not to his personal faults but to those of his fathers, and a sinner's transgressions might be visited not on himself personally but on his descendants. But this view also tended to blunt the bite of personal conscience; it was too easy to minimise one's personal guilt and to underestimate one's personal responsibility for the welfare of the whole; so the prophets found it necessary to react vigorously against it: 'What do you mean by repeating this proverb: The fathers have eaten sour grapes, and the children's teeth are set on edge? As I live, says the Lord God, this proverb shall no longer be used by you in Israel. Behold, all souls are mine; the soul of the father as well as the soul of the son is mine; the soul that sins shall die' (Ez 18:2–4; cf Jer 31:29 f).

But with this, the dilemma becomes acute, for the contradiction between the theory and the fact is obvious; the good are not always successful, sinners very often do not suffer. The book of Job is the most striking protest against the accepted doctrine—the whole book is concerned with this. The author presents Job's friends as defenders of the established position, and they complacently parade the traditional arguments: that if Job suffers misfortune, he must have sinned even if he does not realise it; sinners always suffer, sooner or later, even if it is through their children; and Job indignantly and violently rejects their arguments, leaving himself only with the agony of near-despair (though we shall see later what else emerges from his agony). And the psalms too display the same anguish and bewilderment: 'Fret not yourself because of the wicked, be not envious of wrongdoers' (37:1); 'My mouth shall speak wisdom; why should I fear in times of trouble, when the iniquity of my persecutors surrounds me, men whose trust is in their wealth?' (49: 3-6). We have already considered these psalms in the context of Israel's faith that God is the God of all good; but now we realise that they are often much more than the petulant pleas of spoilt children, jealous of those who have more than they have; they are the outpourings of a genuinely troubled faith. For it is faith, not simply personal comfort which is at stake: 'My feet had almost stumbled, when I saw the prosperity of the wicked. They have no pangs, they are not in trouble as other men are. Therefore the people turn and praise them, and they say: How can God know? These are the wicked, always at ease. In vain have I kept my heart clean '(73:2-13).

Yet this very dilemma opens up a ray of light, and does so by a surprisingly simple turn of thought. By the time that this difficulty arose, by the time of the prophets, Israel was far removed from the simple fellowship of the desert tribes. The conditions of urban living, and trade which was at least as important a factor in their lives as agriculture, meant the introduction of a much more complex economic system; and this in turn gave rise to great inequalities in living standards. The situation is too well documented in the writings of the prophets to need elaboration here: 'They sell the righteous for silver, and the needy for a pair of shoes; they trample the head of the poor into the dust, they lay themselves down by every altar on garments taken in pledge, and in the house of their God they drink the wine of those who have been fined' (Am 2:6–8); 'Woe to those who lie upon beds of ivory, and stretch themselves upon their couches, and eat lambs from the flock, who sing idle songs to the sound of the harp, who drink wine in bowls, and anoint themselves with the finest oils' (Am 6:4–6): 'Hear this, you who trample upon the needy, and bring the poor of the land to an end, saying, When will the new moon be over that we may sell grain, and the sabbath that we may offer wheat for sale, that we may make the ephah small and the shekel great, and deal deceitfully with false balances, that we may buy the poor for silver and the needy for a pair of sandals, and sell the refuse of the wheat' (Am 8:4–6).

But this means that the rich have acquired their wealth at the expense of the covenant laws—sometimes by outright injustice, by dishonesty and malpractice, at the very least by ignoring the basic principle of the covenant, that all Israelites were brothers. Therefore instead of prosperity being a certain sign of God's favour, it is rather more likely that the rich man will be a sinner: 'the man who prospers in his way, the man who carries out evil devices' (37:7); and misfortune too is liable to be the lot of those who have *not* sinned: 'the poor and needy, those who walk uprightly' (37:14). The man who has become wealthy by such unjust means is no true Israelite; he has abandoned the covenant, leaving the poor as the faithful remnant, the true representatives of the covenant people: 'I will remove from your midst your proudly exultant ones, and I will leave in the midst of you a people humble and lowly' (Zeph 3:11 f). The poor are synonymous with 'the people': 'The Lord takes pleasure in his people, he adorns the humble with victory' (149:4).

This is a significant progress in Israel's thought. The connexion between sin and suffering has been broken; and this makes it possible to entertain the thought that suffering might even have something of positive value in it.

Many different trains of thought contributed to this development, and here above all it is difficult to compress them into one simple line of thought. We may begin with the book of Job. Job is remembered mainly for its vehement rejection of the traditional theology, and we sometimes feel that it does not go beyond this—that it simply leaves the whole subject as a mystery, something which simply has to be accepted in blind faith. But this does not do justice to the splendid climax of the book, where the Almighty appears and 'speaks to Job out of the whirlwind' (Job 38:1) with a magnificent account of the marvels of creation and the might of the creator: 'Where were you when I laid the foundations of the earth, when the morning stars sang together and all the sons of God clapped their hands for joy' (Job 38:4, 7). But this is not simply silencing Job with thunder. It is an *epiphany*, an appearance, a revelation of God. Job already knew very well that God made all things; but now he actually sees it: 'I had heard of thee by hearing of the ear, but now my eyes see thee; therefore I despise myself and repent in dust and ashes' (Job 45:5 f). This experience of God is achieved precisely through the experience of suffering. Suffering brings a man to a realisation of his limitation, his need, his dependence; and therefore to a realisation of God on whom he depends. In time of success, in 'the pride of life', when all is going well, we are less able to realise what we really are, we may think we do not need God. Suffering effectively destroys this illusion and brings us back to reality. It is not a misfortune; it is a grace. If a man is crushed to the dust, let him not protest his injured innocence. It is not a question of guilt or innocence, but a question of the real relationship between God and man: 'Even in his angels he finds error, how much more those whose foundation is in the dust' (Job 4:17–19). If man is brought to his knees, this is his proper posture before God.

Suffering is a fire which burns painfully, but it also purges—purges away all complacency and self-sufficiency and leaves a healthy stock for future growth. So Isaiah sees the devastation that is to fall on his country: 'And though a tenth remain in it, it will be burned again like an oak whose stump remains: the holy seed is in its stump' (Is 6:13).

This too is the experience of the prophet Jeremiah. God called him to be a pillar of strength in the land: 'I make you this day a fortified city, an iron pillar, and bronze walls against this land. They will fight against you but they will not prevail against you, for I am with you to deliver you' (Jer 1:18 f). For a man of Jeremiah's temperament, diffident and sensitive, this role did not come naturally, and in the course of his ministry he was conscious of being not so much a pillar of strength as a reed bruised by the opposition and suffering he met with.

But out of his experience of suffering comes the experience of God's power and a new realisation of his own
role: 'If you return, I will return to you: and I will make
you a fortified wall of bronze; they will fight against you
but they shall not prevail over you, for I am with you to
save and deliver you' (Jer 15:19 f).

All of this is not a deduction by reasoned argument. It
is a lived experience. The paradox still remains, a mystery locked to the key of logic. But the very paradox leads
to another step forward. The enigma and the contradiction lead to a reflexion on the 'arbitrariness' of God: 'It
is all one, I say. He destroys both the blameless, and the
wicked. If it is a contest of strength, behold him! If it is a
matter of justice, who can summon him? Though I am
innocent, I cannot answer him. He passes by me and I
see him not' (Job 9:22, 19, 15, 11). The pagans were
familiar with this idea—the Greek dramas are full of it;
and for them there is no explanation other than the whim
of the gods, the 'jealousy' of the gods, *hubris* calling for
nemesis. It leads to despair, disillusion and cynicism; and
the authors of the bible feel the same temptation. But
there is another way of expressing it, another attitude to
the incomprehensible and disconcerting arbitrariness of
God: 'The Lord gives, and the Lord takes away; blessed
be the name of the Lord' (Job 1:21). But this then brings
it into line with a much more familiar thought—the
God who 'kills and brings to life, who brings down to
Sheol and raises up; the Lord makes poor and makes
rich, he brings low, he also exalts; he raises up the poor
from the dust to make them sit with princes' (1 Sam 2:
6–8). This is simply the God of the exodus in a new and
unfamiliar guise. He is the God who brings freedom to
prisoners; should we not experience slavery if we are to
experience the joy of liberation? He brings life from

death: but should we not first experience suffering and death in order to know his life-giving power? 'For God has consigned all men to disobedience, that he may have mercy upon all' (Rom 11:32). 'God chose what is weak to shame the strong; he chose what is low and despised, even what is not, to bring to nothing the things that are. He is the source of your life' (1 Cor 1:27-30).

The ground was now prepared for the most surprising conclusion to Israel's long struggle with the problem of suffering. It was probably the experience of the prophets which contributed most to this. The prophets were not only men who proclaimed God's word; they were totally 'men of the word'; the prophet's whole life, his very being, was consumed by the word. This is why 'symbolic gestures' are so characteristic of the prophets (like Ezekiel, 12:3-7, digging through the wall of his house and coming out with a small bundle of his possessions, to mime the destruction of Jerusalem and the flight of the inhabitants; or Jeremiah, 19:1-10, breaking a jug to show how God would break Israel). Such actions are not meant to be simply an effective, dramatic reinforcement of the spoken word. They *are* a form of the word; the prophet's whole life, what he does as well as what he says, is an expression of the word of God. 'I and the children God has given me are signs and portents in Israel from the Lord of hosts' (Is 8:18); the word of God affects the prophet so totally that it affects even his family relationships—not by anything special that they do or say, but simply in virtue of their being a prophet's children. This is particularly striking in Hosea. He found himself married to an unfaithful wife; but it was his own marital misfortunes which brought home to him and expressed for the people the tragedy of God's love for his unfaithful bride, Israel.

This then casts light on two particularly poignant incidents in the lives of the prophets. God spoke to Ezekiel: 'Son of man, I am about to take the delight of your eyes away; yet you shall not mourn or weep. So I spoke to the people in the morning; and in the evening my wife died' (Ez. 24:15–18). God's message to the people is that they —his bride, the delight of his eyes—will be utterly destroyed; but so well have they deserved this fate that it is not a subject for mourning. But the prophet is called on to experience this message in his own life, by the death of his wife. Similarly, Jeremiah is asked to bear this message of doom, of sorrow and loss, by remaining unmarried (Jer 16:1–4); deprived of the companionship of marriage and the hope of posterity in children, he lives out the fate of Israel.

But then the point is clear: the prophets are asked to suffer indeed (and we remember that for Israel all forms of suffering were an evil—poverty, sickness, persecution, barrenness); but they were suffering because of the sins of the nation. We said earlier that the connexion between sin and suffering had been broken. But this is not quite accurate. The connexion between suffering and one's personal sins had been broken; but it could still be related to the sins of others. And if suffering could lead a sinner to repentance, could not one man's suffering bring relief to another's sin?

The prophet's function already included the task of interceding for the people: 'Have I not entreated thee for their good, have I not pleaded with thee on behalf of the enemy?' (Jer 15:11). And before them Abraham, too, interceding for the people of Sodom (Gen 18:22–33), and Moses, time and again standing between God and the sinful people, represent a very special form of corporate solidarity. And if their words could intercede for

others, why should not their actions too? It was a form of
sacrifice; it was in fact the very essence of sacrifice: 'Sacrifice and sin offering thou has not required. Then I said,
Lo, I come' (40:6 f)): 'The sacrifice acceptable to God
is a broken spirit' (51:17). When people are led to death
'like sheep for the slaughter' (44:11), when Jeremiah felt
that he was 'like a gentle lamb led to the slaughter' (Jer
11:10), it is not only of his submission that he is thinking,
but also of the lamb of sacrifice.

All of this comes to a head in the thought of the prophet known as second Isaiah. He visualises a 'servant of
the Lord' whose preaching meets with opposition, persecution and even death. According to the traditional theology this should have meant that he had incurred the
anger of God: 'We esteemed him stricken by God, smit-
ten and afflicted' (Is 53:4). And indeed it was because of
sin that he suffered, but 'he was wounded for *our* transgressions, bruised for *our* iniquities. All we like sheep had
gone astray, and the Lord laid on him the iniquity of us
all' (5 f). And his sufferings bring atonement for our sins:
'Like a lamb that is led to the slaughter, so he opened not
his mouth; he makes himself an offering for sin. Upon
him was the chastisement that made us whole, and with
his stripes we have been healed. He bore the sins of many
and made intercession for the transgressors, and the
righteous one made many righteous' (7, 10, 5, 12, 11).

This is the end of the long road which began with—
and never abandoned—the simple conviction that God
is good. It only remains for Jesus to live in practice this
ideal.

None of the psalms reach this peak of theological
awareness; but nevertheless there is a genuine spirituality
of suffering in the psalms. It is an attitude of humility,
learnt by humiliation. The pride of life, and easy self-

confidence, has been purged by suffering; and 'suffering' and 'meek' become practically synonymous: 'O Lord, thou wilt hear the desire of the meek, thou wilt incline thine ear to the oppressed' (10:17). So their prayer sometimes takes the form of quiet trustfulness: 'My heart is not lifted up, my eyes are not raised too high. I have stilled and quieted my soul like a child quieted at its mother's breast' (131:1 f). This is not just the submissiveness of a passive temperament; it needs an act of will, 'I have calmed my soul'. And more often it results in loud complaint; after all, suffering *is* an evil, and passive acceptance of it or even stoic forebearance is not a christian attitude. Our Lord himself did not hide his feelings in his suffering: 'My soul is very sorrowful, even to death' (Mk 14:34); and at the moment of his death he found no better way of expressing his desolation than one of these psalms: 'My God, my God, why hast thou forsaken me' (Mk 15:34, Ps 22:1). The psalmists are usually even more vociferous. Genteel resignation would be as out of place here as artificial gentility in the social order: 'Do not go gentle into that good night'. They badger and browbeat God; they flourish their misery before him like an oriental beggar displaying his sores and deformity: 'My eye is wasted from grief, my soul and body also. My life is spent with sorrow, my years with sighing; my strength fails because of my misery and my bones waste away' (31:9 f): 'There is no soundness in my flesh because of thy indignation, there is no health in my bones, my wounds grow foul and fester, I am utterly spent and crushed' (38:3–8). They are not ashamed to be importunate; they are beyond the humiliation of a rebuff. They not only plead with God, they demand his help as of right: 'Rouse thyself! Why sleepest thou, O God?' (44:23). They remind him of his past mercies, they call to mind his power, they appeal to his own reputation: 'Deliver us for thy name's sake; why should the nations say, Where is their God?' (79:9 f).

But it is always appeal to God; it is never merely defiance hurled into the empty air. They wait on the Lord, with patient longing, 'more than watchmen for the morning' (129:6). Their suffering even makes them more attentive to him: 'As the eyes of servants look to the hand of their master, so are my eyes on the Lord till he have mercy on us' (123:2). Their experience of God is the counterpart of their experience of suffering. They are as helpless as sheep; but they are the sheep of God's pasture (74:1; 79:13)—the 'little flock', to whom the Lord says: 'Fear not' (Lk 12:32). To him, they say: 'Lord, to whom shall we go? Thou hast the words of eternal life' (Jn 6:68). 'I kept my faith, even when I said, I am greatly afflicted. I said in consternation, Men are all a vain hope' (116:10).

These are real prayers. They are the prayers of the destitute, the deprived, the failures. It is not romanticised or idealised. They are the prayers of ordinary people at odds with ordinary life, and very often getting the worst of the encounter. These are real prayers of life.

Ps 133

There is no point in even trying to mention all the psalms which express sorrow or yearning. We will just deal with two psalms which represent different aspects of the thought we have been dealing with. Ps 133 is a very short poem—just three phrases—on brotherly love. The author gives two comparisons and we may begin with these; it is like oil, like the dew. It is completely alien to biblical thought to make a sharp distinction between material and spiritual, between body and soul. God is the living God; all good comes from him and is the expression of his goodness. The fertility of the earth is a sign of divine blessing, the blessing of life—of divine life, 'life for evermore'. It is the rain which makes the crops grow; but even more strikingly the dew—appearing so unexpectedly after a cloudless night—speaks to us of God's gift. So Israel rejoices in the grace of a rich land and a rich life: 'May God give you of the dew of heaven and of the fatness of the earth' (Gen 27:25). This grace—oil, oil of gladness, oil of strength—is then used in the consecration of the priest; and the thoroughly oriental language ('running down onto the beard, running down onto the collar') must not distract us from the real point: that the richness of divine blessing is abundantly poured out on the priest whose function it is to offer Israel's worship and gratitude for the gift.

God is present in our lives, in the gifts with which he surrounds us; he is present in our worship; but all of this is of no avail if he is not also present in our love for one another. This is the real sign and sacrament of God's presence amongst us.

Ps 22

Ps 22 is a typical example of the laments of the psalter. In particular, it is a clear example of a common feature of such psalms—the abrupt change from pitiful, almost desperate plea (1–21) to confident, joyful gratitude for deliverance (22–31). Obviously the psalm was not composed or recited in the midst of suffering, as appears at first. One might almost describe it as 'emotion recollected in tranquillity', except that the tranquillity achieved does not dispel the memory of the reality of the anguish.

The expression of distress is heart-rending; but as so often in these psalms, it is difficult to see the precise source of it. Real though the emotion is, it is not simply a personal lament; it is a prayer in the name of all who suffer, a prayer of suffering humanity.

What is most deeply distressing is not the physical suffering which seems to be implied in 22:14 and 16, for example; nor the criticism and contempt with which he is assailed (22:4 f); but the sense of utter desolation and isolation when God himself is absent. He is driven back on himself, and in that final refuge where he should find God, he finds nothing. This is particularly shattering for one who had known the confidence of God's presence and had every reason to trust him. His very existence was a gift of God and pledge of his loving care (9 f). Above all, he was born into a people whose whole history was marked by God's loving, saving presence (5 f); God was enthroned in their midst, not only in the ark of covenant, but in the heartfelt praise of the people who had known his love (3). But now, instead of the security of the shadow of his wings, he is surrounded and buffeted by a swarm of troubles (11).

Yet even in this desolation, he cannot help calling on God, on the God who is absent; he still calls on '*my* God'. This fluctuation between despair and hope is characteristic of deep suffering—the feeling that there is no one to turn to, and the urge to call on him.

And so he returns to the bad dream of his sufferings. They are described in the nightmarish terms of a fevered brain (12–18), partly taken from the language of mythology (cf p 91 f), but expressing also the idea that our suffering is opposed to God's plan, that there is something demonic in it; it is like Paul's words about his sufferings: 'I fought with the beasts at Ephesus' (1 Cor 15:32): 'Our struggle is not with flesh and blood, but with principalities and powers, with the world rulers of this present darkness, with the spiritual hosts of wickedness in high places' (Eph 6:12). Underneath all our suffering, no matter how 'normal' and prosaic, and no matter what else we may have to say about its positive value, there is the reality of something wrong, the mark of a disordered world, of something alien to the absolute goodness of God.

And then suddenly comes the realisation of deliverance (22–31). And just as in the expression of his suffering the psalmist was expressing his personal experience but also the experience of all who suffer, so in his joy he calls on the community to join him. Statements like 'God is good', 'God loves us', are completely unreal if they do not express something in our experience; it is difficult to see what possible meaning they can have if that goodness and love are not seen in our lives. They are so often absent from our own experience that it is all the more important that they should be seen somewhere in human experience. The psalmist is bearing witness to the goodness and mercy of God in his own experience. It is a different sort of 'argument' from that of the philosophers or theologians who attempt to prove God's existence and his attributes, but it is much more real. How can we possibly worship and thank God if we have not known his love? The psalmist calls on us to join him in his jubilation.

Moreover, this is the very nature of God—it is not an accidental, casual, isolated act of benevolence; it is the expression of what he is. It is the expression of his being which transcends time and place. So the psalmist thinks not only of his friends, of his fellow-Israelites, but of all men; the same love and mercy and power to save is for 'all the ends of the earth, for all the families of nations' (27 f), and even ages to come (30), and even ages gone by, even the dead (29). The outstretched arms of a loving God embrace the whole of suffering humanity.

1. We do normally pray more frequently and more fervently when we are in need. Is this a rather shameful sign of our self-seeking? What do the psalmists describe as 'suffering'? Only great tragedies like death or serious sickness, or does it include such 'minor' irritations as headaches and occasional failures?

   2. Do the psalms adopt a consistent attitude to the problem of evil? Should we?

The wisdom literature

Michael Smith

Introduction to the wisdom literature

12/11/76

All men must seek wisdom; it is available to all, but can be totally possessed by none; this thought underlies the disparate group of books in the old testament classified generally as wisdom writings. Preoccupied at first with the problems of successful living, they witness to a long tradition of study, reflection and argument in Israelite schools. Before the exile, formal education was generally restricted to the sons of the rich, young men destined to become administrators or court officials (cf Dan 1). A more general education was provided by parents. In later times, as the ideal of equal opportunity gained wider acceptance, the schools took their pupils from all classes, but kept many of the earlier methods and motifs. Throughout Israel's history the wisdom books witness to the international interests of the wise men; the schools took shape when Israel became a kingdom, probably in the reign of Solomon, and were strongly influenced by the ancient Egyptian pedagogic tradition. The wise men were truly international, their experience broad and their teachings eclectic; they muted the fierce nationalism of Israel's early faith.

The wisdom writings, particularly Proverbs, Sirach and Ecclesiastes, are sometimes pictured as basically secular, self-interested and practical, concerned with the details of daily living rather than the vision of faith. They seem to lack concern for the great themes of Israel's sacred history; covenant and promise, election and law: hence many have disparaged their religious value, seeing them merely as collections of rather obvious common-sense maxims. Setting aside the development visible in these books from Proverbs to Sirach, from Ecclesiastes to Wisdom, this narrow classification overlooks two important features of the writings. Their creation-faith and unified conception of the world meant that all experience had profound religious value; also the sages' concern with the 'right way of doing things' was not mere conformism but stemmed from the conviction that this is the way to God, because it harmonises with the pattern of God's creation in man and the world. The wisdom writers were also interested in history, especially in the context of present decision. They applied their traditions to changing political and cultural milieux, in line with the various needs of different communities—the emerging nation in post-exilic Palestine in Proverbs, the conflict with aggressive hellenism in Sirach and Wisdom. The wisdom movement was at once traditional and innovative; new insights were constantly being brought to bear on age-old problems and their traditional solutions.

Above all, the schoolmen valued wisdom, understanding and insight. At once God's gift and the product of human experience, wisdom was seen as the ability to discern the basic patterns of reality, drawing conclusions about correct behaviour in accordance with this God-given pattern. At first probably influenced by the Egyptian notion of *ma'at*, or the harmony of things, the idea of wisdom expanded, became regarded as an attribute of God and agent of his creation, and as an independent entity formed the basis for some new testament theologies of incarnation. Insight came through experience, reflected upon, accumulated and handed on by the sages. The first, fundamental and necessary condition for the young scholar was desire for wisdom; without patience and courage in the search, its secrets would always remain hidden. The sages knew that the way to wisdom is never easy, for some men only have experiences, while others gain experience. The esoteric element in wisdom speculation later found a home in apocalyptic literature; but the notion that practical wisdom is hardly learned and not to be disseminated indiscriminately remained constant in the tradition.

The methods and concerns of the sages were firmly grounded in the human condition. The problems of retribution for just and unjust, of suffering, of the value of righteous living and fruitful human interaction preoccupied them most, but their interest in the conditions for successful living was not limited merely to the demands of enlightened self-interest. Humility was constantly emphasised; the man who counted himself wise was least likely to be so in fact. Wisdom was grounded ineradicably in deep religious faith in God's power and transcendence. Only he knows the full pattern and purpose of creation; the ambiguities, apparent contradictions and anomalies of the world exercised the sages' power to comprehend but never destroyed this faith. They resisted the temptation to impose order on reality, and attempted to gain some insight, a penetration they recognised as limited, into a world whose coherence they accepted in faith. Nor were the sages mere dispensers of traditional insight; Job and Ecclesiastes manifest in different ways the extent of the debate in the schools on the crucial question of life's purpose, with the realisation that righteous living, accepted not through passive conformity but in total faith, did not necessarily imply success and prosperity 'under the sun'. Their search for ways to reconcile the diverse justice of man and God called for even deeper insight and faith.

Proverbs, riddles, parables, allegories and vivid metaphor are all utilised by the sages to express and encapsulate their search for insight. Thus they preserved the richness and mystery of the world, as these many-layered symbols and sayings crystallise a wealth of insight. 'A proverb is the wisdom of many and the wit of one', and armed with these sayings the pupils of the schools were enabled to give some structure to the many questions of life. Like all proverbs, these sayings are essentially openended, and this makes them still of value for us. The boundaries of living are limited by man's nature, which in its deepest reaches, especially in relation to God, has not appreciably altered its limits throughout his history.

The wisdom books are once again coming into their own in the appreciation of scholars. In our man-centered age, when the advance of technology has still not solved the problems of humanity, true human insight retains a special value. The purpose of life, the discernment of good, the acquiring of wisdom, the mystery of human relations; the answers to all these questions must begin with the insights of the sages. The possibility of life after death was argued in terms similar to the current debate; the human drama of Job summarises all who suffer, showing the utter inadequacy of the wrong kind of religious sympathy. The problem of faith was never avoided; the wisdom writers knew the temptations to cynicism and scepticism, and the difficulty of maintaining faith in the face of fallen expectations. Wisdom never grows old; the echoes of their teachings in the proverbs and parables of the new testament, in the christologies of

John and Paul and the practical sense of James are the bible's own witness to this fact. The ethical teaching of the new testament is largely that of the old, where it was concentrated in the wisdom books. Many biblical proverbs are still used in everyday speech; if these books are studied with the care and attention accorded them by the ancient scholars, they still provide a rich fund of warm human insight.

Book list

R. E. Murphy *Seven Books of Wisdom* Milwaukee 1960.

R. B. Y. Scott *Proverbs, Ecclesiastes* London 1965.

D. Kidner *The Proverbs, Introduction and Commentary* London 1964.

E. Jones *Proverbs and Ecclesiastes* London 1961.

E. Jones *The Triumph of Job* London 1966.

A. & M. Hanson *The Book of Job* London 1953.

N. H. Snaith *The Book of Job* London 1968.

J. Geyer *The Wisdom of Solomon* London 1963.

J. Reider *The Book of Wisdom* New York 1957.

B. Vawter *The Book of Sirach* New York 1962.

E. T. Ryder *Ecclesiastes* London 1962.

Job
Introduction

The book of Job counts among the greatest of literary masterpieces, and is justly famed for its imagery, perception and piety. At one level, it deals with the problem of the just man's sufferings; more profoundly, with the whole of man's relation to God. After the trauma of exile, when a collectivist interpretation of the covenant formulas proved increasingly inadequate to comprehend the nuances of faith in a pluralistic, unsettled environment, the personal nature of man's contract with God needed further elaboration. Ezekiel (18) stressed personal responsibility for one's actions; the sages went one stage further, maintaining that prudent and righteous living produces the fulness of life, the fulfilment of the promises for the wise individual. Compared with the solid assurance of Proverbs, Job's perception of man's state before God is nuanced and subtle, and witnesses to a high degree of critical evaluation of traditional formulas in the schools. The book takes the form of a disputation, a court of justice, at once a court of enquiry and a court of appeal.

The saga of Job, composed probably in the fifth century, is built on an ancient wisdom parable illustrating the problem of retribution, of which 1:1–22, 42:11–17 form the kernel. The main argument is worked out in the first series of dialogues (3–31), where Job disputes the standard doctrine of the schools. He is a recognised wisdom teacher himself (4:3–5), and the dialogues indicate the constant process of evaluation and examination that must have formed an important part of the school's activity. The three counsellors try to bring Job to acknowledge that his misfortune is due to his sin; Job consistently maintains his basic innocence, calling on God to justify his afflictions. Elihu's speeches (32–37) were added later; they take more account of Job's arguments and indicate a certain development in the schoolmen's theodicy, bringing forward some new arguments. Yahweh's speech concludes the drama (38–41); he interrogates Job, reminding him of the discrepancy in their knowledge, and the absurdity of his request for complete understanding of his situation—Job makes basically the same mistake as his 'friends' by expecting to understand his situation completely.

Job accuses his friends of giving pat answers, of trying to reduce God to their own dimension, of substituting ritual penitence for personal contact with God. The standard answers of the schools cannot satisfy his search for meaning to his suffering, especially their automatic association of suffering and sin. Suffering is not always punishment, nor do those who abandon the ways of God always receive their expected deserts. This leads Job to question the whole purpose of life—if there is no reunion with God after death (this is considered but rejected), then what is the point of his afflictions? Correction and discipline are insufficient explanations, the only answer lies in accepting the realities of life, trusting in God's power to bring forth good from this paradox.

Against the formal, uncritical doctrines of the counsellors, Job continually appeals to personal experience.

He suggests that their glib diagnosis might be different if they were in his situation—he even challenges God to meet him on his own ground. His prayer is answered, and in personal contact with Yahweh, in his vision of God caring for the whole of his creation, he finally finds an insight if not an answer. He probes the limits of faith, attempting to understand yet always aware that understanding must eventually dissolve into mystery. The author's courage in pushing to the boundaries of faith is balanced by his delicate awareness of the limitations of all human knowledge. With sympathetic irony, he shows that the standard doctrines of the schools are not wrong, but rather too rigid. Even Job's own protestations of innocence become less certain as he begins to realise the extent of God's concern.

For the modern reader, Job offers no easy answers to life's problems, but the book describes, uniquely in the bible, one man's search for meaning within the context of faith. False comfort, easy-sounding answers, and petulant pessimism are all rejected; agonising self-doubt and inner uncertainty prevent overemphasis on selfish concerns. Suffering, misfortune and loss befall the pious; prosperity rewards the pagans as well as the chosen people. The schools were preoccupied with the problem of explaining God's random favour to pious Israelites, but the book of Job attacks the larger problem of the purpose of faith. The multiplicity of names for God show that the author did not restrict himself to Israel's faith, as the God he seeks is the God of all. If Job provides no complete solution, he at least raises all the significant questions and leaves the way open to genuine faith.

1

Prologue
Job 1:1–2:13

Job 1:1–5. The stylised archaic introduction sets the scene for the subsequent drama. Job is portrayed as a great nomadic patriarch, surrounded by flocks and family; also as the quintessential religious man—punctilious to the point of scrupulosity, but concerned with para-genuine, interior piety.

Job 1:6–12. In the heavenly court, Yahweh is represented as an oriental monarch, surrounded by his chief advisers, one of whom was Satan, the adversary—devil's advocate rather than devil. Yahweh points to Job as the exemplar of the just (1:8), but the Satan questions whether Job's piety is genuinely disinterested. 'Does Job fear God for nought?' means for no return on his investment (1:9)—this question is one of the main concerns of the book. He could be pious simply because he is prosperous. Yahweh allows Satan to strip Job of his possessions, in line with the common theory that temporary deprivation is a test of virtue.

Job 1:13–22. Job loses his wealth and his family, but passes the test—he mourns but continues to praise God.

Job 2:1–6. This repeats the scene in heaven; the Satan's scepticism ironically is shown to be 'without cause' (2:3). using the same Hebrew word as 1:9. This time the

Satan claims the test did not go far enough; only when a man's own body is afflicted does his true nature appear.

Job 2:7–10. Job's virtue is probed to the depths, for self-interest can still be unaffected when it is only others, even the closest, who suffer. All hope seems to be lost, and Job's wife adds her plea to curse God and die; she reacts as the Satan predicted. Job rebukes her, continuing to assert God's right; he passes the test completely. Job's total reliance on God is necessary for the subsequent drama to retain its force; he represents the extreme case of the genuinely holy man who suffers horribly yet remains faithful.

Job 2:11–13. When Job's friends hear of his state, they come, with the best of intentions, to comfort him; they mourn for him as for one dead and wait expectantly for him to speak.

2
Dialogue with the three friends
Job 3:1–31:40

This section begins and ends with a soliloquy by Job (3:29–31): in between come the friends' nine interventions, all followed by Job's replies. These take the form of a series of lamentation poems in traditional style; an appeal to God, followed by a description of the sufferings, then a plea for deliverance. The friends offer consolation by joining in Job's appeal, but because of a basic understanding, their consolation soon becomes accusation. They see Job's sufferings as resulting from sin and expect him to repent, whereas Job maintains, not so much that he is sinless, but that he is unaware of having sinned. The friends' rigid doctrine of retribution leads them to accuse Job of defying God, which only adds to his anguish. He would still like to believe that God loves him.

Job 3:1–26. Job's first soliloquy

Job 3:1–10. Job curses the night of his conception and day of his birth, implying that the life God has given him is worthless. Conception and birth, traditional signs of the fertility of God's promise, should be times for joy, but if they result in the life Job has to live, they are worthless.

Job 3:11–19. Job begins to question the purpose of such a life. It would have been better to die young, missing all hope of the promise; at least he would have shared the grey existence of Sheol with the rich and the great. God is made to appear like a slavemaster; at least Job would have a measure of peace in the grave.

Job 3:20–26. Job questions God directly—why does he give a gift that is essentially purposeless, cutting off all chance of growth? Job's sufferings are fundamentally interior—he can have no peace as long as he cannot understand.

Job 4:1–5:27. Eliphaz' first speech
The senior counsellor is confident that he has the answer to Job's question.

Job 4:1–11. Eliphaz is slightly disconcerted by Job's problem—Job has been a teacher in the schools, so he must know the answer: gently Eliphaz tries to lead Job to accept it. Already Eliphaz has missed the point, for the standard doctrine of retribution is just what Job has begun to question. The experience Eliphaz appeals to (4:8) is too much an expression of faith in this doctrine to carry much weight. He acknowledges Job's piety (4:6), which should give him confidence; he will later deny it (15:4).

Job 4:12–21. Eliphaz' appeal to experience is backed by secret revelations, given in dreams. The later schools tried to claim a supernatural authority, similar to that of the prophets, for their teachings; they also emphasised their esoteric nature, as they considered not all men equally capable of understanding. The secret is revealed—no man is guiltless. Job's claim to innocence is unfounded.

Job 5:1–7. Job's lament is useless; the saints have no power to help him; his impatience will only destroy him, as it has his sons (5:4). Job's fate is thrown back in his face; suffering is man's own fault.

Job 5:8–18. Eliphaz' practical advice is for Job to admit his sin and pray confidently for deliverance. God always helps the poor, he also chastens the pious for their own good (Ps 94:12).

Job 5:19–26. Two numerical poems list the seven troubles from which Job will be freed (5:20–22), and the seven blessings he will receive (5:23–26). This teaching is absolutely certain, proved by experience and revelation; all that remains is for Job to put it into practice (5:27).

The author's irony is obvious; Job never sought material blessings, only understanding. The basic paradox lies in the fact that the normal rules cannot apply to Job for he was never unjust; God's action was arbitrary, so there is no way he can earn the recovery of his family and fortune.

Job 6:1–7:21. Job's reply

Job 6:1–13. Job protests at the way Eliphaz misunderstands him. His suffering cannot be approached in the abstract, with a material formula; it is too vast and too personal for him to be appeased by the doctrine of God's discipline, which he feels as torture (6:4). He would rather be annihilated than face unfeeling advice; then he would know he had not deserted God, but purposeless patience asks for too much (6:11–13).

Job 6:14–30. Job asks for true sympathy from his friends. He thought they would refresh him, but they are as dry as a *wadi* in summer. He did not ask much of their friendship (6:22–23); only that they understand his point of view, and not confront him with wordy principles (6:24–30).

Job 7:1–10. Job contrasts Eliphaz' confident optimism in 5:17 ff with the reality of his situation; like that of a slave or common labourer. Because it is so wretched, his life seems worse than pointless. In 7:7–10 he addresses God, whom he has always known as a friend. Previously God had looked kindly upon him; Job prays that he will find him again before it is too late.

Job 7:11–21. Instead of making his prayer one of repentance, Job decides to speak out. Job is only a man, not the chaotic mighty sea, yet he is tormented night and day; if God does not want to help him, why cannot he leave him alone? He quotes Ps 8:4, an exclamation of gratitude at God's care for insignificant man, with bitter irony—it is beneath God's dignity to subject man to prolonged scrutiny. The categories of retributive justice cannot apply between man and God (7:20); while Job had always considered God his friend, he now seems to be his enemy. Surely God can afford to pardon him, before it is too late?

Job 8:1–22. Bildad's speech

Job 8:1–7. Bildad presents the doctrine of retributive justice in a more extreme and narrow form than Eliphaz —not even God himself can deflect its course. The principle takes precedence over the person even in God, who is never unjust. Job's children must have sinned—their punishment is complete, but Job can deliver himself and find renewed prosperity by repentance and righteous living. This too God must reward.

Job 8:8–10. Bildad reinforces his naive and rigid view by appealing to the ancients—evidently a younger man, he thus offsets Job's greater age.

Job 8:11–22. The fate of the godless is outlined (8:11–19)—they can have no enduring hope, even though they prosper for a while, for they may be destroyed in an instant. In contrast, Job will prosper if he accepts this advice. Again, the author's irony appears in the fact that this promise will be fulfilled, but it will be the friends who are put to shame.

Job 9:1–10:22. Job's reply

The form is the same as previously; Job reacts to his friend's advice, soliloquises on his own situation, then prays to God.

Job 9:2–24. Job takes up Eliphaz' comment in 4:17, acknowledging that man has no right against God. This is not because God is always in the right, as though there were some principle of law operating between God and man, but because of God's power—what he decides is necessarily right, no one can gainsay him. This makes all justice a mystery, and the friends' concept entirely inadequate (9:2–12). Yet to the afflicted man who still considers himself innocent, such justice can only seem arbitrary anger, for he has no right of appeal, and can only wait for unearned clemency.

Job 9:25–35. Job soliloquises on what might happen if he did pretend all was well. Even if he abandoned his appeal, the fact of his affliction indicates God has prejudged him, so affected repentance would be useless. Arbitration is impossible now; only if Job's affliction, the sign of his guilt, were removed could he plead with any confidence.

Job 10:1–22. Job 'prays', asking God for the real reason for his suffering. In desperation, he accuses God of

enjoying being vindictive (10:3), or of being mistaken
(10:4), or of being jealous even of man's limited happiness (10:5–7) in a perverse commentary on the effects
of applying human categories of justice to God. He
knows God fashioned him with loving care, and for this
he is grateful—but what kind of life is this if it turns to
persecution? (10:8–17). It would have been better if he
had never been born (10:18–22, cf 3:1–26).

Job 11:1–20. Zophar's speech

Zophar is the most intransigent of the three—he under-
takes to defend God's wisdom rather than his justice, a
mystery which he demystifies by professing to understand it. He distorts Job's own attitude, for Job did not
claim to be absolutely blameless, only to be unaware of
any fault commensurate with the degree of his sufferings.
God's ways are mysterious (11:7–10), but Zophar knows
them, Job's affliction proves his guilt (11:11)—for the
author such pretended wisdom is true foolishness (11:12).
Zophar appeals to Job to renounce the wickedness he is
unable to define, repeating the promise of automatic
peace and prosperity. He puts more emphasis on the
alleviation of Job's spiritual distress, but chides him for
desiring death—this is also a sign of sin (11:13–20).

Job 12:1–14:22. Job's reply

Job 12:1–25. Job retorts to his friends' appeal to wisdom
with heavy sarcasm—what they say is obvious, but their
platitudes have missed the point at issue, the reason why
the innocent man should suffer and be mocked. God
certainly does govern the world, he does punish and reward, everything is subject to his controlling wisdom—
these are general principles obvious to all men of faith,

even to plants and animals (12:7–10). But this merely demonstrates his supreme and inviolable power; any inevitable connexion with man's sin remains to be proved (12:13–25).

Job 13:1–12. The real problem lies in the particular application of the principles; this is what Job is concerned with. He knows the standard doctrine of the schools as well as his counsellors, but he alone dares to go further, to question God, and put his wisdom to the real test (13:3). The friends would do better to keep silent, for they must distort the truth to maintain their narrow conception of God's activity, and consequently distort God by their rigid anthropomorphism (13:7–12). God will not thank them for defending him thus; his wisdom and knowledge cannot be confined by their limitations.

Job 13:13–28. Job asks for time to defend himself, mixing fear at the outcome (13:13–15) with courageous confidence in his vindication (13:16–19). His relationship with God has always been devoutly personal, so now he pleads, on the basis of this, for a respite from his anguish and also for an answer from God (13:20–22). Besides being a personal appeal, Job's speech is also a legal defence; he has to presuppose God is his opponent, and that there is common ground on which they can argue. This marks Job's own presumption; even though he recognises his weakness, God seems to be persecuting him.

Job 14:1–22. Job returns to his theme of life's limits, asking God not to scrutinise man so strictly. He briefly explores the possibility of life after death, which would enable him to endure (14:14–17) his present sufferings in hope of being reconciled to God and restored to his friendship, but the contrasting metaphors of the budding stump (14:7–9) and the crumbling mountain (14:18–19) underline his conviction that the present life is all man's hope (14:10–12, 20). The thought that his sons may prosper offers little comfort to the man who must face pain and oblivion himself.

1. Does the notion of God testing man for his own good have any value for our religious life?

2. Do we still tend to see suffering as a result of sin?

3. To what extent is our image of God necessarily irrational?

Job 15:1–35. Eliphaz' second speech

Job 15:1–16. Eliphaz now adopts a threatening tone, attacking Job's temerity in refusing the proffered counsel and encouragement. Job is not really wise at all (cf 4:3–6)—his attitude proves his sin, for Job's daring in addressing God so bluntly contradicts the piety, reverence and respect for God so much emphasised in wisdom schools. One may conjecture that this was often confused with respect for the teacher, for Job also rejects sound advice (15:9–10). Job is not the first man born, the mythical *Urmensch* endowed with all wisdom (cf Ez 28:11–19, Prov 8:22–26); rather like all men, since he must acknowledge his weakness and sin. Wisdom's slightly pessimistic view of human nature, already apparent in Proverb's stress on discipline, correction and respect, underlies this section; repentance and righteous living should be sufficient consolation (15:11, a reference to Eliphaz' first speech).

Job 15:17–35. Consolation turns to threat—Job, who 'bids defiance to the Almighty' (15:25), will surely suffer for this most serious of his sins. Eliphaz clothes his threat with all the panoply of wisdom's authority, he represents the tradition of the ancient heroes and saints, guardians of Israel's purity.

Job 16:1–17:16. Job's reply

Job 16:1–17. Job answers these accusations in equally direct language. He denounces his opponents; Eliphaz (16:2–3), the three together (16:4–11), and God (16:12–14). Eliphaz is himself full of wind (16:2, cf 15:2), giving useless comfort (16:3, cf 15:11). It is easy for them to deliver their platitudes, as they do not experience Job's agony; their need to speak masks their own incomprehension. Instead of comforting they have become Job's enemies; their unfriendly attitude is a further sign of Job's punishment. God seems to stand behind them, though Job feels he has done penance enough.

Job 16:18–21. Innocent blood cries to God for vengeance; Job asks the earth not to stifle this cry. God seems to be Job's murderer; but against all appearance Job maintains his faith, calling on God to hear his cry. He has given up on his counsellors, instead he asks God to treat him justly as would any true human friend.

Job 16:22–17:16. Even if Job does not expect to live, he does want vindication. He asks God to find him an advocate, to defend him against his counsellors' lack of understanding (17:4). If they continue in the same vein, supporting the prosperous with their complacent doctrine, it is their pupils who will eventually suffer (17:5). Job's situation is scandalous (17:6–8), but they misunderstand the nature of the scandal. Job rejects their unfounded optimism (17:12, cf 11:17); he knows there is only death ahead, but hopes for an answer from God, not mere restoration of his property (17:13–16).

Job 18:1–21. Bildad's second speech

Bildad rebukes Job, mocking his search for understanding; the friends' comfortable wisdom contrasts with Job's impotence. The bulk of the chapter describes the fate of the man 'who knows not God' (18:21). Job is a heretic, an apostate and infidel—the curse he refused to utter is seen as the reason for his affliction.

Job 19:1–29. Job's reply

Job 19:1–12. Job cannot understand why the counsellors attack him so bitterly—he may have erred but this should not affect them (19:4). They seem to protest too much; but while they look for the reason for his suffering in Job's sin, he knows that it results from God's deliberate action (19:5–6), nor is it based on justice (19:7). Further, God has shut Job off, isolating him with enmity.

Job 19:13–22. This isolation is reflected in all Job's acquaintances; from the farthest to the closest, they avoid him like the plague. All interpersonal life is lost, all he has left is the barest physical existence; he is even forced to plead with his unfeeling friends to show him some pity.

Job 19:23–29. Job still believes in himself and in God; though he must die, he wants his plea for vindication indelibly inscribed in rock. He believes he will have a vindicator, a *go'el* or kinsman who will plead his case for him; presumably it is to be the living God himself (cf 16:19). Although Job will be in *she'ol*, he apparently hopes to have a vision of this process. Job's faith breaks the bonds of pessimism; his friends, who persist in seeing the cause of his troubles in Job himself, will then be subject to God's judgement.

Job 20:1–29. Zophar's second speech

This repeats, more angrily, the theme of the certain retribution of the wicked stressed by Bildad in ch 18. Zophar, alone among the friends, hears Job's censure, and is shaken for a moment (20:3), but insists all the more strongly on the principle of sudden and immediate disaster for the wicked; Job's former wealth must have been illgotten (20:6–11). These two speeches frame Job's central confession of faith; the author implies that their unyielding insistence, rather than Job's impatience, leads to eventual despair.

Job 21:1–34. Job's reply

Job 21:1–26. Job moves on to the attack—ironically, he now offers to console his friends, certain he will shock them. He insists on the facts—the godless do not always perish—even Job himself is disconcerted by this discovery (21:6). There are good men who seem to feel no need of God, yet they enjoy the same prosperity promised the just believer (cf 5:20–26). It seems as though God rewards the godless; the standard answer that such a man's punishment is visited on his children is unsatisfactory, for if justice is operative he should feel the punishment himself (21:19–21). The counsellors accused Job of trying to be wiser than God; in fact they presume to judge in his name, even when he apparently does not conform to their doctrine (21:22–26).

Job 21:27–34. Even their appeal to future dishonour shows how false their 'comfort' is; they assert the godless are always punished in the safety of their schools, but dare not do so to their face. They search out important and successful men, and honour them after death, even if they are wicked. They judge by appearances, by the world's values in the world.

1. Does the concept of man's wickedness stem from preaching rather than theology?

2. How shocking is Job's complaint? Does it reflect faith or lack of reverence?

Job 22:1–30. Eliphaz' third speech

Job 22:1–11. Eliphaz now turns to specifics, appalled by Job's audacity. Wisdom's whole purpose is to benefit man, as God is above the struggle; he cannot be held to account, nor can he be said to punish Job for piety's sake. Therefore Job must be guilty of the standard sins, all the exploitations denounced by the prophets (Is 58:6–7). Ironically Eliphaz' catalogue of Job's purported cruelty manifests his own misconception, the deeper cruelty of the man who seeks holiness without compassion.

Job 22:12–20. Eliphaz suggests Job's denial of wisdom's principles blankets God behind the clouds; also the 'good pagans' (21:14–15) were finally destroyed in the flood (22:15–18).

Job 22:21–28. Eliphaz, as God's spokesman (22:22), exhorts Job to be humble, to abase himself; then God will be ready to hear and reward him, then he may bargain on 'equal' terms (22:28), confident in his righteousness.

Job 23:1–24:25. Job's reply

Job 23:1–7. Job laments his inability to reach God; all he wants is to understand, and he knows God would answer his arguments gently, as his faith overcomes his former bitterness (9:13–21, 13:14–27).

Job 23:8–17. God remains inaccessible to Job, but watches like Big Brother—if Job's sufferings are only a test, then he has nothing to fear, but he is terrified they are quite arbitrary. He repudiates Eliphaz' accusations, however, he has always kept the laws.

Job 24:1–12. Not only does God not punish the wicked (21:7–17), he does not always recompense innocent victims of injustice.

Job 24:13–24. This section does not seem to belong to Job's speech. 24:13–17 is a short thematic paradigm; murderers, adulterers and thieves all work in the dark. 24:18–24 describe the fate of the wicked in terms similar to those used by the friends.

Job 24:25. Conclusion of Job's reply.

Job 25:1–27:23. Final speeches of Zophar and Bildad; Job's reply

Textual corruption and dislocation has obscured the basic pattern in this section, and no rearrangement is totally satisfactory.

Job 25:1–6. Bildad's third speech returns to the themes of God's absolute dominion and man's impurity (cf 4:17–19, 15:14–16).

Job 26:1–14. Job's reply sarcastically rebukes Bildad's profound platitudes (26:2–4); Job agrees with all he has said and expands his praise of God's power, which extends from inert *she'ol* to the whole of creation.

Job 27:7–23. Zophar's third speech finally gives up all hope for Job—everything he possesses will be lost. Job in reply (27:1–6), insists on his innocence and integrity, the absolute value of his conscience.

Job 28:1–28. Hymn in praise of wisdom

This poem, similar in certain respects to Prov 8, Sir 24, interrupts the dialogue, and was probably composed separately. In the context, it lays the groundwork for Job's final speech, giving the lie to Eliphaz—no one knows God's wisdom and power (cf 15:17–19). Man may explore the earth, and find many of its secret treasures in his search (28:1–11); but priceless wisdom remains hidden (28:12–19). Its secret is known only to God (28:20–27), who had revealed it to man in concrete terms (28:28, cf Prov 1:7; 8:13).

Job 29:1–31:40. Job's final speech

Job sums up the case for his defence. He contrasts his former peace and prosperity (29) with his present misery (30); then swears he is innocent of any crime (31).

Job 29:1–25. Job describes his former state, as a great sheikh, emphasising his friendship with God (29:2–6) and his beneficent wisdom, respected by all (29:7–17). He expected this situation would always continue (29:18–20); men would always listen respectfully to his words of comfort (29:21–25).

Job 30:1–31. Now all is reversed; instead of respecting, the poor and the young mock him, he is outcast even from the outcasts of society (30:1–15). Worse still, God has rejected him; he does not answer Job, but hounds him to death (30:16–23). Job knew the bitterness of unsympathetic friends (6:14–23, 19:21 f), yet he always showed concern for the afflicted; surely God will do likewise for him (30:24–31).

Job 31:1–40. The 'oath of innocence' was an accepted legal procedure in disputed or uncertain cases. The defendant would swear to his innocence, invoking God's curse if he should lie. Although Job's power had made him to some extent above the law, he emphasises his concern for the lowest, and genuine interior virtue. Job signs his oath (31:25) and confidently demands vindication (31:36–37).

1. *How justified is Job in saying that in God might is right?*
2. *Does any man have any rights before God?*

3

The speeches of Elihu
Job 32:1–37:24

Job 32:1–6. The four speeches of Elihu, the son of Barachel, separate Job's oath of innocence and demand for a hearing from God's reply. This section, coming outside the dialogue and not mentioned in the introduction, was presumably added later by a different author. It does not add anything new, but stresses the purifying and educative value of suffering. Mention of Elihu's youth and self-importance perhaps parodies a younger school of wisdom writers who were dissatisfied both with the doctrine of strict retribution and Job's demand for complete understanding.

Job 32:6–22. Introduction

Job 32:6–14. Elihu rebukes the friends, who could not answer Job; but is confident he possesses the spirit of true wisdom. He can refute Job, there is no need to wait for God.

Job. 32:15–22. The spirit compels him to speak (cf Am 3:8, Jer 20:7–9, Mic 3:8), and he does not intend to mince words.

Job 33:1–30. Elihu's first speech

Job 33:1–11. Job may fear to face God (9:17, 34), but

he need not be afraid of Elihu (33:1–7). He repeats Job's arguments; that he is innocent (9:21; 10:7) yet God treats him like an enemy (10:17; 19:11).

Job 33:12–33. Elihu rebukes Job; he intends to show him how God has in fact answered his second point in two ways. The first is the terrifying dreams Job referred to (7:14, cf also 4:12–21); these are intended as a warning (33:12–18). Secondly, God speaks to man through suffering; which is not so much a sign of sin as a means of humbling man, disposing him to hear the angel's call to prayer and repentance, the sure way to communion with God (33:19–28).

Job 34:1–37. Elihu's second speech

Job 34:1–9. Elihu takes up Job's first point, his conviction of innocence. He aligns Job with the atheists (22:15–17), who saw no need for faith (34:9); Job's protestations are thus an attack on God's providence, insinuating that he does not reward the just; Job at least would deny that he always does so (9:22 f).

Job 34:10–30. Elihu states the correct principle; God requites man according to his deeds (34:10–11). He cannot act unjustly, or the universe would fall apart (34:12–15); he is the supreme governor, above all other authority, hence necessarily just (34:16–20). He cannot be called to account for his judgements, for he is the one truly all-seeing judge. Even when he does not seem to act, man has no right to say he is remiss (34:29).

Job 34:31–37. Elihu describes the repentant sinner, who accepts his suffering and turns to God (34:31–32). If Job complains sinners go unpunished, what of divine mercy? Job accused God of acting arbitrarily towards him; does he mean to say God should always punish sin, as did his friends? Job must choose—if he allows God's mercy, God must also be free to punish for a purpose—he cannot have it both ways (34:33). Elihu knows he has scored a point; he wishes Job should be punished to the limit, to teach him a lesson (34:34–37).

Job 35:1–16. Elihu's third speech

Job said he might well have sinned, for all the harm it did God (7:20); Eliphaz maintained man's good deeds bring God no benefit (22:2–3). Both are right, man's actions affect only man (35:8). This is not to say God is indifferent, for when the poor suffer, they often complain to anyone but God; human pride blocks out penitent prayer (35:9–12). God hears their cry but does not answer because it is inappropriate (35:13); still more is this true in Job's case, for he should know better than to make demands on God (35:14–16).

Job 36:1–37:24. Elihu's fourth speech

Job 36:1–4. Elihu has so far shown that God does speak to man, that as creator he cannot be unjust, and that he is not indifferent or unaware. He now sets out wisdom's principles describing God's relation to man.

Job 36:5–23. God ultimately restores justice (36:5–7); temporary affliction serves to turn the just from proud self-reliance (36:8–10). It provides a moment of truth, a test; those who listen will prosper, those who do not will perish (36:11–12). 36:13–15 comments on this last principle; 36:17–23 applies the warning to Job. The text of 36:16 is hopelessly corrupt.

Job 36:24–25. Therefore man cannot question God, only praise him.

Job 36:26–37:13. A hymn in praise of God's majesty. Thunder, lightning and rain all manifest God's power; he also uses them to punish or reward (36:31, 37:13, cf Pss 8, 18, 28, 104, Wis 10–19).

Job 37:14–20. Elihu asks Job ironically if he can do likewise. These questions prepare for those Yahweh asks himself. Job should instruct him, if he knows so much, how to make a case against God; in fact, he is as much in the dark as anyone else (37:19–20).

Job 37:21–24. Traditionally, the theophany came from the north (Is 14:13, Ez 1:4, Ps 47:2–3); Elihu departs as abruptly as he came, but his last words introduce God's intervention.

   1. What are some of the limits of the notion of God's providence?

   2. Does prayer have to be perfect to be answered?

4

The speeches of Yahweh
Job 38:1–42:6

Job has continually called on God to answer him, and finally God shows himself. He stands as Job's accuser, but shifts the whole dispute on to another plane, making no mention of any sins Job may or may not have committed. Instead he poses a series of rhetorical questions; the extent and depth of his knowledge and care for his creatures contrast with Job's concern for himself. God watches over the whole natural world— he established all its definition. The hymn brilliantly expresses the schools' reverence for creation's complexity, and dominant belief that this was ordered and controlled by Yahweh. The perpetually interlocking patterns of creation's mystery all lead directly to God.

Job 38:1–40:2. Yahweh's first speech

Job 38:1–2. God speaks directly to Job, answering his plea (13:22, 23:5, 30:20), from the whirlwind, the traditional site of the theophany (Ps 18:8–14).

Job 38:3–38. He contrasts his 'counsel', the plan of his providence, with Job's groping questions, using the inanimate world as example. Was Job present at the creation (38:4–15), does he know the interlinking arrangement of the universe (38:16–24), could he make it work, give the necessary orders (38:25–28)?

Job 38:39–39:30. The animal world provides further proof. He describes eight creatures, all of whom he, rather than Job, provides for and protects. Even the warhorse, who cooperates with man the most, gets his spirited nature from God (39:19–25).

Job 40:1–2. Job is challenged to reply.

Job 40:3–5. Job's reply

Job had always insisted that God must answer his just plea; now he has done so. Job's incapacity is revealed, he acknowledges that he has no further questions.

Job 40:6–41:26. Yahweh's second speech

Job 40:6–14. Here Yahweh takes the themes of his first speech one stage further, treating the mystery of his relations with man. He challenges Job to establish an absolute moral order himself, since he has accused him of distorting justice (9:24, 19:6, 27:2). Job has no power to regulate retribution, therefore he has no right to challenge God's methods.

Job 40:15–24, 41:1–34. The references to Behemoth and Leviathan, monsters beyond the control of man (presumably based on the hippopotamus and crocodile), indicate the extent of God's power. The underlying reference is to the mythical chaotic powers (Job 3:8, Ps 73:14) conquered by God in creation. There is an irrational, irregular element in the world, over which man has no power, but this is also part of God's plan for creation.

Job 42:1–6. Job's final reply

Job's quest is finally ended, but not in the way he expected. There is no answer, the problem of suffering is not solved, but neither is it shelved. Job did demand too much in demanding to know the answer; he now acknowledges his presumption (42:3–4). The friends had told him much the same but impersonally—now Job's faith in God's personal care is vindicated as he gains a vision of his love. Secure in this love and acceptance, he is at last able to repent peacefully, not even needing to rely on his innocence. Personal faith alone can sublimate the impersonal problem.

5
Epilogue
Job 42:7–17

Job 42:7–9. Just as Job has learned to deal gently with reality, not to demand complete answers to insoluble problems, so God deals gently with the unsympathetic counsellors, who also attempted to make God over in the image of their principles. The mercy shown them refutes their arrogance and lack of insight.

Job 42:10–17. Job's friends and family return, he again enjoys life to the full. The author does not totally abandon the principle of material recompense; he is concerned to show that material goods are a poor indicator of one's standing with God. Job would agree with the author of Ps 73—'For me it is good to be near God' (Ps 73:28).

1. Did Job in fact win his argument with God?
2. How ironic was his promise of repentance?

Proverbs
Introduction

The Book of Proverbs, in purpose and form, could be described as the Hebrew equivalent of those anthologies of English poetry once common in every grammar school. It is the oldest of the wisdom books, but was given its final shape sometime after the exile, probably in the fifth century. The editor reworked two ancient collections of the most primitive kind of Hebrew poetry, to which he added smaller appendices written by foreign sages, and wrote a prologue in a more elegant and developed style, recasting and expanding the whole direction of wisdom's tradition. The book is attributed to Solomon, a sign of the school's reverence for tradition. Pseudonymity was a commonly accepted literary device, but the attribution is more than usually apt in the case of Proverbs. The two central sections, Prov 10:1–22:16 and 25:1–29:27, probably originated well before the exile; the first being attributed to Solomon and the second to 'the men of Hezekiah', who reigned from 715–687. The literary wisdom tradition originated in court circles, and was probably introduced to Israel by Solomon, whose contacts with Egypt and the southern regions are well attested (1 Kg 4:29–34). As the kingdom took shape schools were needed to educate upper-class young men to become administrators, overseers, or advisers to the king. Such schools had existed in Egypt since the third millennium, designed to train young men in the subtle arts of managing men and affairs.

The needs of the reconstituted nation were somewhat different. The returning exiles, led by Ezra the scribe and Nehemiah, found their land occupied by aliens, their culture and traditions largely neglected. Side-by-side with the re-establishment of law and worship (Ezr 7:25), they recognised the need for a strong educational system to combat the widespread immorality and injustice produced by the uncertain political and cultural situation. The traumatic experience of the exile had shaken faith in Yahweh's inevitable protection of his people; the concept of community had become rather tenuous. Men were concerned with their individual security, and the wisdom tradition, with its emphasis on the individual, complemented this trend and attempted to direct it aright, relying on the age-old concept of retribution— blessings and prosperity attend the wise, while the foolish will be denuded. But the lessons of the prophets, who had often conflicted with the wise men of the past, the king's advisers (Is 19:11-12; Jer 18:18), had been taken to heart, and broadened the notion of wisdom. In the prologue, it is equated with virtue, and also the law of Yahweh; fidelity to the law is the sole guarantor of prosperity.

The school's teaching methods relied heavily on memory and application. Discipline was strict, and the need for restraint and moderation heavily emphasised. The oldest collections use the simplest form of the *mashal*, or saying, a one or two-member couplet. Concise, skilfully fashioned, they made insight memorable and accessible. While many of the maxims in these collections provide advice for courtiers and counsellors, others reach back into the tribal, family heritage of Israel. The earliest educators were the patriarchs and chieftains, and the schools maintained the link with this older tradition in the traditional 'My son . . .' form of address used by the teacher. The smaller collections use other favourite forms, riddles and numerical proverbs, while the editor of the prologue fashioned long elaborate artistically structured poems, using allegory and extended metaphor.

This development in form coincides with a development in the understanding of wisdom, which originally described the quality of skill, dexterity or artistry in judgement or execution. Allied with discernment, particularly the discernment of the order or harmony of the world, wisdom became, as well as a capacity for man, an attribute of God, who had established this harmony in creation. The ethical perspective of wisdom was strengthened and deepened, as the predominantly secular concern of the early collections was more and more suffused with this creation-faith. Even in the early sections what looks to us like self-interest is often simply a reflection of the sages' unified world-view; all man's purposes and actions are under the hand of God. The sages affirm the value of the created world, seeing it as the reflexion of God's activity.

6
The first collection
Prov 1:1–9:18

Prov 1:1–5. Title and purpose

Proverbs as a whole is attributed to Solomon, the patron
and exemplar of Israelite wisdom. It is a textbook or
handbook for use in the schools, but is by no means merely a primer. While the teachings are intended primarily
for the young and unlearned, it offers much of value to
the more advanced. All grades of proficiency studied together in the schools, under the guidance of the teacher,
and the wise may acquire the art of guidance or 'steer-
ing', the sympathetic and subtle ability to influence men
and events, the acme of practical wisdom. The theory
and practice of wisdom are distinguished, their various
nuances outlined by a series of complementary terms.
Wisdom (*hokmah*) basically describes any outstanding
human skill; discipline (*musar*) the quality of restraint so
necessary to curb impetuous youth and avoid misunder-
standing; insight (*bina*) the ability to discern true and
false, to separate the valuable from the worthless, to see
beneath appearances. Practical wisdom (1:3–5) consists
in living in accordance with the demands of right living
(*tsedeq*), in the ability to make prudent and proper decisions (*mishpat*), in total honesty (*me'sarim*). Shrewdness,
resourcefulness and flexibility must replace naivety and
ignorance.

Prov 1 : 7. The basic principle

This couplet recasts the whole wisdom tradition, equating wisdom with 'fear of the Lord'; reverence for God whose power and presence underlies all man's effort. The Hebrew word used here means both 'beginning' and 'acme', as all knowledge grows from true piety and also culminates in it. The sages traditionally began their instruction by expounding wisdom's merits, exhorting their pupils to seek understanding. Here wisdom and folly are contrasted, and given a new meaning; folly is lack of reverence and awareness, the shallow scorn and arrogant self-reliance of the unenlightened. The search for wisdom requires discipline, here in the sense of persistence, spurning temptation; the shortsighted will not be likely to submit to the necessary restraints.

Prov 1 : 8–19. Warning against seduction

The sage begins by warning his pupils to pay attention to his teachings; to reject the transitory benefits offered by those outside the schools, evil companions looking for easy ways to get rich. The speech of the wicked is similar in form to Wis 2 : 10–20, and the sage's caution relies on the ingrained principle that those who make violence a way of life will suffer its effects in themselves (cf Mt 26 : 52), as sin is its own punishment. The wise man takes the long view; like the wary bird who escapes the trap he can see the net spread before him. 1 : 16 is a gloss from Is 59 : 7, where the prophet attacks false counsellors. The sages are extremely conscious of those who scorned their teachings, and while their opponents' methods were probably not quite as drastic as they are represented they are conscious that it is but a short step from reliance on expedient self-interest to overt violence.

Prov 1:20–33. Wisdom's invitation

Following the initial warning against false counsel, wisdom invites all men to begin the elusive search for her. Wisdom is given personal qualities in many different contexts; here she acts like a prophet. While the teachings of the wise lack the prophetic urgency and involvement in Israel's history, the choice to return to wisdom is as utterly crucial as the decision for repentance. The sages had to contend with the common problem of all committed teachers; what seemed vital to them was regarded by many as trivial, stupid or beneath contempt. The apparently complacent determinism of the sages did not stem from unconcern but from conviction. They were conscious that they offered the result of generations of experience, the distilled wisdom of history, summed up in the basic principle that no man escapes the inherent consequences of his choices and actions. Only if these are properly guided is security or peace possible. No one is competent in his own case, immune from the seductive demands of self; every man must be willing to learn, to listen to the voice of true wisdom.

Prov 2:1–7:27. Discourses of the sage

These six chapters consist of an ordered discourse of seven groups, each of about twenty-two verses, in which the sage expounds wisdom's blessings, and warns against some common obstacles.

Prov 2:1–22. Introduction

This opening lesson-poem, of six verses, arranged in two groups of four-line verses followed by a three-line verse, introduces the major topics the sage wishes to consider.

The second and third verses emphasise wisdom's positive benefits, service of the Lord and a well-ordered life, and the fourth and fifth warn against the advice of irreligious men and the charms of seductive women, two major obstacles in the young man's search for wisdom.

Prov 2:1–4. The basic and absolutely necessary disposition is the desire for wisdom (Wis 6:12 ff, 7:7 ff; Sir 6:18), and docility and diligence in the search. Wisdom should be sought at least as eagerly as buried treasure; the sage cleverly turns the get-rich-quick dream of all ages of men to emphasise wisdom's deeper and more durable rewards.

Prov 2:5–8. These qualities provide the necessary ground for wisdom, which while it must be sought eagerly by man is ultimately the gift of God. The mutual interaction of reverent man and generous God, the basis of the covenant relationship (cf Ex 20:20), is expressed in wisdom terms. Wisdom, like the law, protects honest men; only those who are sincere in their dedication to God, their initial commitment, are sure of his protection (cf Wis 1:5).

Prov 2:9–11. Wisdom, the personal possession of the trustworthy man (cf Sir 4:11 ff), protects him against all adversity (cf Mt 10:20; Lk 21:15; Ac 6:10) for she is beyond the reach of his opponents.

Prov 2:12–15. The 'men of perverse speech', often a synonym for apostate Jews, oppose the traditions of Yahwistic religion. They own no allegiance to God, placing all reliance on their own efforts. In the unsettled conditions of post-exilic Palestine, their example was especially abhorrent to the sages as they tried to rebuild religious consciousness in their pupils.

Prov 2:16–19. The strange or alien woman appears frequently in this section. Solomon had been led astray by his foreign wives (1 Kg 11:8), and the problems of religious and racial purity, as well as marital fidelity, were especially important as the Israelites strove to refashion their national and religious identity in a land where the alien presence was pronounced (cf Ezr 9–10). Besides the practical problem, the warning has definite overtones of covenant fidelity (cf Ex 20:14, 17; Mal 2:14); adultery with foreign women was a communal as well as personal offence. Infidelity leads to death, the death of the spirit consequent on loss of Yahweh's promises; whereas the sages promised life, a complex of prosperity, peace and productive fellowship. There is as yet no idea of any future life.

Prov 2:20–22. This verse summarises and concludes the poem, recalling the deuteronomic vision of a land inhabited by the wise where everything is directed by order and reason, whence the enemies of the promise have been removed. It is an ideal land, but while the territorial link is rather tenuous, the community of the just, and only the just, constitutes the new nation. They are the true heirs of the promise, but they possess the land only in terms of promise.

Prov 3:1–35. The way to get wisdom

This chapter expands the themes introduced in Prov 2: 5–8. Two main lessons or instructions (Prov 3:1–12, 21–35) emphasise respectively dedication to Yahweh as the source of wisdom (cf Prov 2:5–6), and wisdom's guiding and protecting power (cf Prov 2:7–8).

Prov 3:1–12. First instruction—God and wisdom

Six verses of two couplets each with an injunction fol-

lowed by explanation, or description of the consequent
reward, make up this lesson poem. Parents and teachers
alike desire their sons to make a success of life, to experience and enjoy its full benefits. Education, attention and
dedication to the words of experience provide the key
(3:1–2). But more is needed for truly successful life;
ḥesed we'emet loyalty and faithfulness, describe God's
covenant-relation to Israel (Ex 34:6), and form an ideal
pattern for man's attitude to God and his fellows (Hos
4:1). True wisdom is based on devotion to Yahweh; it is
not found through the perception or skill in argument so
highly prized in non-Israelite schools. Prov 3:7 is similar
to Is 5:21, where the prophet attacked the pragmatic approach of the king's advisers, insisting on the priority of
faith (Jer 9:22–23). The prologue manifests the spiri-
tualisation of wisdom; in the earlier Prov 26:5–11, 16 to
be 'wise in one's own eyes' indicates stupidity rather than
stubborn unbelief. Good and evil have an absolute
quality, dependent on the demands of faith; they no
longer simply indicate the circumstances of success. In
Prov 3:9–10 expectation of the good life does not follow
simply from diligence and discipline; it also depends on
liturgy and worship. This is the only instance in Proverbs
where there is any mention of the cult; and indicates the
way in which ancient wisdom was becoming suffused
by Yahwistic faith. Prov 3:11–12 adds a characteristic note of caution; prosperity and health do not
come automatically even to the just. The problem
of retribution, so central to their thought, was never
completely solved by the Jewish sages. Here the author
uses one of the standard explanations; the sufferings
of the just are God's discipline, and indicate his love
rather than displeasure (cf Deut 8:5; Job 5:17; Heb
12:5–6).

Prov 3:13–18. Hymn in praise of wisdom's blessings

A hymn praising wisdom as the source of all good. The form 'Happy is the man' is in some ways similar to the new testament beatitudes (Mt 5:1 ff); it is a proclamation of praise, a definitive and creative description of the truly complete man. Here he is the one who at first finds and finally holds fast to wisdom. The poem has a climactic, ascending note; the gradual deepening of wisdom through a man's life is brought out in widening comparisons, first of the treasures wisdom surpasses, then of her positive benefits. The 'tree of life' is a common image for a vital, intensely-lived, completely full life; there are no apparent overtones of life after death.

Prov 3:19–20. The basis for faith in wisdom was its role in God's creation, ordering the universe. The passage perhaps marks a transitional stage in the development of wisdom's persona, from human perspicacity to divine attribute (cf Prov 8:22 f). The analogy of wisdom stresses the derivative character of human insight; its full scope and range is proper to God alone.

Prov 3:21–35. Second instruction, wisdom's protection. The first section (3:21–26) emphasises 'sound wisdom and discretion', namely prudence, resourcefulness, finesse and competence, as well as the importance of concentration. Alertness indicates vitality, and provides the best protection against the sudden shifts of fortune so disconcerting to the unwary or undisciplined (Eccl 9:12). The whole passage is couched in terms of Yahwistic piety, the secure road where there are no hidden traps. Prov 3:26 makes this explicit—the truly wise, therefore pious and just man can rely on the assurance of Yahweh's protection, as well as his own sagacity and self-control, in time of trouble.

Prov 3:27–30 warns against selfishness. In christian terms, the level of altruism is perhaps minimal, but the injunctions probably derive from advice to young administrators. Good government is rarely served by pettiness or procrastination. In this context, the emphasis lies more on general good fellowship, avoiding tensions and divisions likely to place too much strain on the nascent community. Exploitation and unnecessary litigation threatened the unspoken framework of mutual trust necessary for communal security.

Prov 3:31–35 concentrates on the 'man of violence', who will stop at nothing to get his own way. The sages were always aware of the danger such men posed to their teachings, as their pupils, anxious to get ahead, would be likely to envy the success of the unscrupulous, and find it difficult to understand any absolute need for justice, when the wicked so often prospered (cf Wis 2–5; Job 21: 7). The sage counters with a series of contrasts: the honest, righteous, humble wise man, the friend of God, compares favourably with the devious, unjust, arrogant fool whom God and man both spurn. Prov 3:34 (in the Septuagint version) is emphasised in early christian ethical teaching, cf 1 Pet 5:5; Jas 4:6, 1 Clement.

Prov 4:1–9. A father's advice

Prov 4:1–5a show wisdom's antiquity, originally handed down as a living tradition from father to son, then from teacher to favourite pupils in the schools, where the ancient mode of address was retained. The young pupil is not encouraged to branch off on his own; only the teacher, who has lived, plumbed and made his own the tradition passed on to him can speak with personal authority, because he summarises the accumulated insight of countless generations. This sense of tradition, combined with the demands of Yahwistic piety, formed the basis of wisdom's authority. Prov 4:5b–9 stress the utter importance of acquiring wisdom. While it comes only gradually and not without struggle, as is implied by the victory symbols of the crown and diadem, it demands persevering allegiance, and in return bestows harmony, protection and peace.

Prov 4:10–27. The two ways

These two poems (4:10–19, 20–27), link back to wisdom's third blessing (Prov 2:12–15), the power to deliver from evil. The metaphor of the two ways, or way of the left and way of the right hand in the Septuagint, appears consistently in ethical instruction into new testament times (cf Gen 18:19; Is 12:23; Pss 1:1, 18:21, 25:9; Jer 18:11; Ez 3:8; Jon 3:8; Zech 1:4; Mt 21:32; Rom 3:17; 1 Cor 12:31; 2 Pet 2:15, 21, *Didache*). The poems open with the characteristic call for attention and docility, and reminder of wisdom's rewards. The promise of life in 4:13, 22–23 resemble Deut 30:20 where the law gives life to the true Israelite; here it is the wise man's instruction. The way of wisdom is unhampered, unobstructed; it ensures self-confidence, and provides the key to difficult decisions. In contrast, the wicked are consumed with evil; addicted to violence, they find in it no satisfaction. It is useless food that does them no good. The just wise man is always honest and direct (4:15, 24–27); singleminded and purposeful in the search for wisdom and justice, he will be successful in life.

Prov 5:1–23. Warning against adultery

The fourth discourse takes up and expands the warning in Prov 2:16–19, building on standard and universal advice for the young, which dates back to the Egyptian instructions. The teacher emphasises its practical nature; the young man is especially likely to be deceived by appearances in this context, but the sage stresses reality, experience, and the inevitable consequences of self-deception.

Prov 5:1–14. Beware the seductress: the warnings refer especially to dealings with prostitutes, whether they be cult-prostitutes or simply available women. At first they appear to offer untold delights, seductively flattering the ambitious male ego; but the end result is remorse, the bitter experience of one's own stupidity. This woman leads to death—the metaphor refers to the complete estrangement from society, the gradual loss of all worthwhile relationships resulting from association with her. As the prostitute stands outside the boundaries of society, so does the man who associates himself with her; he cannot commute from one milieu to the other. The woman of pleasure is totally unpredictable, a creature of whim, yet she can lead a man by the nose, so he cannot see reason. This is totally abhorrent to the sage's reverence for order and structure in life.

The wise course is to avoid such women completely; the young man should never place himself in any situation where he is liable to fall victim. The prostitute is merciless because the very nature of her calling demands that all the elements of worthwhile human relationships be excluded; and the financial consequences can be disastrous. It is expensive to keep a mistress, and compensation to a wronged husband can be ruinous. The section concludes with the too-late lament of one who did not listen sufficiently to the initial warning, a true-to-life example of the consequences of folly.

Prov 5:15–23. Exhortation to fidelity: the sensual imagery of this section underlines the contrast between fidelity and infidelity, and serves to emphasise more strongly the concrete, real effects of genuine human love. Water was precious in the east; necessary for life and fertility, it was not to be wasted. The blessings of children and companionship, a genuine sharing of self, are the fruits of constancy. The man who is double-dealing in love cannot escape the eye of God, nor the consequences of his own actions; he necessarily forgoes any knowledge of true human companionship and love.

Prov 6:1–19. Four poems on folly

Prov 6:1–5 warns against entanglement with money-lenders. In common with many intellectuals, the sages tended to look down on the more mundane aspects of the business world; farming was a more gentlemanly occupation. Here the young man is warned against letting his name be used as surety for others; while the warning is common in Prov (11:15, 17:18, 20:16, 22:26–27, 27:13), the sages also recognised the need to help others in financial difficulties (Sir 29:20). If a man has become entangled, self-esteem must not stand in the way of swift extricating action.

The sages were great students of nature's ways; the ant offers a pointed example of industry (Prov 24:30–34; 26; 13–16; 30:24–25). She needs no exhortation but works steadily to provide for future needs. The sages seem to reserve some of their most savage strictures for the lazy; the careless, day-to-day, unthinking life of the dreamer inevitably results in deprivation.

The double-dealing insincere schemer, whose gestures even are confusing, reaps the reward inherent in his own deceit. The dissension he creates, as well as his own duplicity, ultimately tears him apart.

The numerical proverb is a common literary device in the bible (cf Deut 32:30; Am 1:3; Mic 5:4; Ps 62:12; Sir 25:7; 36:5, 19); it is used repeatedly in Prov 30. Peace and harmony is a fragile treasure; disorder in the community is most abhorrent to the sages and administrators. Men who combine resourcefulness and intelligence with active self-interest deny everything most necessary for good relations among men, hence they incur the Lord's hatred.

Prov 6:20–35. Further warnings against adultery: the general introductory admonition (6:20–23) followed by a specific warning illustrates the basic pedagogic pattern in the schools; the teaching of the law, and corrective discipline or self-restraint are the essential qualities required. In contrast to the previous warnings, Proverbs here concentrates on the dangers of adultery with a married woman. This is far more dangerous than an affair with a prostitute who can be bought for a moment, who is also usually a lower-class woman, for the married woman will want to uproot a whole life. Flirting can be fun but is dangerous because of its inherent dynamism, above all a man must be careful in the beginning, as covering up the traces later on is rarely successful. Stealing bread in need is a small crime compared with stolen affections; while that is considered no shame, the adulterer is totally disgraced and loses all he has worked for in life.

Prov 7:1–27. The adulteress

The basic instructional pattern recurs; introduction (7:
1–5), theme in the form of a novel (7:6–23), conclusion
(7:24–27). The description of the harlot's tactics prepares a contrast with wisdom's invitation in the following chapter. The seduction summarises the common
temptation facing the young man searching for wisdom.
The sage's sympathetic scorn, contrasting the young
man's callow bemusement with the woman's assurance,
reflects the frustration of one who has seen too many fall
into this trap (7:26). The mention of the fulfilment of
the woman's vows (7:14) and the absent husband suggest that this woman is not a common prostitute, more
probably a rich man's wife fulfilling a devotion to Aphrodite; the sage may also be delineating common excuses
to trap a man, with religious services providing a 'chance'
meeting when the husband is absent. The consequences
of folly are outlined; love in luxury is short-lived but its
effects endure much longer (7:24–27).

Prov 8:1–36. Wisdom's call

This chapter consists of seven strophes of five couplets,
the first six of which are grouped in pairs, and finished
with a summary exhortation.

Prov 8:1–11. Wisdom calls the young: wisdom takes to
the street, but addresses men directly and openly, in contrast to the deceptive tactics of the harlot. Wisdom here
is presented as apostolic, she presents her message to all
men, almost like a prophet. This procedure perhaps reflects an expansionist, anti-elitist tendency in the post-
exilic schools (cf Sirach, Ecclesiastes). In some circles
wisdom was considered to be a secret jealously guarded

and never communicated to the unlearned, but here wisdom is presented as a teacher, explicitly seeking the callow, unformed young man, to bring him insight and the capacity for discernment, worldly know-how and intellectual judgement. This discernment is not merely practical, for it is rooted in wisdom's own integrity; true wisdom is utterly sincere. There is an implicit contrast with superficial advice that may deceive the young man; it is in this sense that wisdom is superior to silver, gold and jewels. These are not disparaged, in fact have immense value, as long as they are used according to wisdom's value system.

Prov 8:12–21. Wisdom's competence: these verses illustrate something of the development of the notion and sphere of wisdom in Israel. The basic appeal is to old wisdom with her skill in guiding the affairs of men; she gives the shrewdness, practical insight and confidence indispensable to successful politics. Wisdom is the source of real power, the 'power behind the throne', and also shows the way to genuine prosperity. Wisdom guides the counsellor, but the original political emphasis is given a moral quality by the addition of 8:13a, 'the fear of the Lord is to hate evil'. The intellectual discipline of the early schools is transformed into moral discipline, as the ancient imperatives are allied with Yahwistic piety.

Prov 8:22–31. The origins of wisdom: wisdom's practical advantages are transcended in this section; the editor bridges the transition with his note in 8:22. Wisdom is placed in a cosmological context; her authority stems from her priority to all creation as the pattern of God's activity. Her architectonic function emphasises the vast range of her intellectual competence; the author here is writing with the same apologetic intent as in the preceding sections but for a more sophisticated and discriminating audience. The language is similar to that used to describe Yahweh as the architect of creation in Is 40:12–17, 28–31, where the prophet reinterpreted the language of older wisdom and applied it to Yahweh. Here there has been a further development within the schools themselves, as wisdom is personified and takes on the character of Yahweh's attributes, which was carried further in the later writings of Sir 24:1–21; Wis 7:22–8:1; Bar 3:9–4:4, stressing wisdom's activity at creation. Wisdom's birth from God suggests a certain precedence and divine affinity which makes her superior to the rest of creation. As God's child, his 'darling', wisdom plays before him at the creation, and expresses the inherent goodness of the world and of man; the sages seem to envision an *urzeit* when wisdom was natural to all, when there was no need for discipline and restraint.

Prov 8:32–36. Conclusion: wisdom addresses the young men as a teacher his pupils; discipline and instruction are the only way to life, they found the ultimate fulfilment of a man's religious duties. The wise man's pupils gathered for instruction at the door of his house; so they should wait for life-bringing wisdom; the door of the harlot's house in contrast is the gateway to sheol.

Prov 9:1–18. The banquets of wisdom and folly

The seven pillars represent wisdom's perfection; her house, or way of life, is represented by the proverbs in 9:7–12. Wisdom's maidens contrast with the harlot; they reflect wisdom's integrity, and address themselves to raw young men, inviting them to school, to the promise of maturity. The meal itself is modelled on yet contrasted with the cultic meals of Aphrodite worship; while there was no explicit cult of wisdom in Israel, the festive abundant nature of the meal suggests the richness of the life wisdom offers. There is no sacramental element here, but the symbolism of the food of instruction and life to which men are invited is common to both testaments; cf Is 25: 6, 55:1–5; Mt 22:1–14; Lk 12:37.

Six independent proverbs, 9:7–12, castigate the scoffer, the arrogant man who rejects wisdom's invitation outright; there is no sense in arguing with cynics (Prov 15: 12, 19:25) as their unattractive self-centredness eventually drives everyone away (9:12).

The foolish harlot contrasts with wisdom; she likewise calls to the simple and unlearned, but her meal of bread and water compares unfavourably with the meat and wine of wisdom, all the more because it is stolen. Its attraction lies only in its deceptive appearance, but all folly offers in fact is shameful oblivion.

1. In what ways can wisdom be taught?

2. How much does our school system concentrate on teaching wisdom?

7
The other collections
Prov 10:1–31:31

Prov 10:1–22:16. The first Solomonic collection

These independent two-line sayings, with the second
stich usually a motive-clause or a parallel elaboration,
summarise the best of ancient Israelite wisdom. They are
arranged in random fashion, occasionally linked by
catchwords, assonance or alliteration, as a mnemonic device. Chapters 10–15 offer pragmatic advice, while 16–22
have a more obviously religious tone, but the whole is
suffused by the total world-view which gave all human
action and interaction moral value.

The ideal man is depicted positively and by contrast
negatively, in the standard opposed categories of wise and
foolish, virtuous and wicked, rich and poor, industrious
and slothful, expressing the whole gamut of human life-
styles in their constantly shifting perspectives. A kind of
religious self-interest predominates, as the truly wise man
is prudent (13:16; 14:15–16), sober (14:30), cautious
(11:15) and restrained (10:19; 14:17). Order and stabil-
ity are necessary for genuine growth (16:28–29); hard
work is necessary to gain prosperity (12:9, 24; 14:23;
19:15). Wealth rewards (16:20) and protects the wise
(10:15; 13:8), but virtue is better still (10:2; 11:28, 15,
16; 16:16).

In his relationships with others, the virtuous man is always honest (11:1; 12:19–22; 19:5; 20:10); there can be no justice without this (11:1). More than that, he is generous (11:24–26; 19:17) and forgiving (10:12; 15:1; 17:9), not driven by selfish interests (22:16). He finds delight in his wife and family (12:4; 15:20; 18:22), shows concern for his children by strong discipline (12:1; 13:1, 24; 19:18; 22:6); and is respectful of proper authority (16:12–15).

In his relations with God, the wise man is motivated by fear of the Lord, the awesome awareness of his power which leads to a true understanding of life (14:27; 15:33; 19:23; 22:4). God's providence decides man's fate (16:1–9, 35; 19:21); but God too is just, rewarding the virtuous (10:3, 27) and punishing the wicked (11:21). Later thinkers would question the aptness of this doctrine, but the earlier sages were concerned to stress humility (10:12) and submission.

Prov 22:17–24:22. Sayings of the wise

This collection resembles the Egyptian *Wisdom of Amen-em-ope*. More developed in form, using four line verses, it is particularly concerned with the education of promising young administrators and scribes. The sage moderates the desire to get on at any cost; they must not oppress the poor, must choose their companions carefully, and reverence tradition. They must be careful not to be over-impressed by the rich, and beware of avarice and sensuality. 23:29–35 depicts vividly the folly of drink, another trap for young players (23:19–21; 31:4–7).

Prov 24:23–34. Further sayings of the wise

These miscellaneous sayings stress industry and sincerity; honesty builds friendship (24:26).

Prov 25:1–29:33. Second Solomonic collection

This collection is attributed to the men of Hezekiah (716–687), who brought prosperity and peace to Israel by his religious reform (2 Kg 18–20). Chapters 25–26 consist of longer poems, offering practical advice, and using vivid similes and metaphors drawn from nature. The other chapters use the two-line saying, with frequent use of antithesis, and have a more religious tone.

Prov 30:1–31:31. Miscellaneous collections

Prov 30:1–14. The words of Agur. Agur's poem stresses the limits of human knowledge in contrast to God's wisdom (30:1–4); various additions elaborate on this theme. 30:5–6 is perhaps a scribal instruction implying that revelation is limited to the sacred books; 30:7–9 is a prayer for honesty and detachment, and 30:11–14 describes the arrogant.

Prov 30:15–33. Numerical poems. These use images from nature to highlight human qualities, with the staccato phrasing giving a climactic effect to the final line. Verses 17, 20, 32–33 comment on the sayings.

Prov 31:1–9. The sayings of Lemuel. Proverbs mentions the maternal instruction (1:8; 6:20; 15:20); wisdom was never considered an exclusively masculine preserve, and the king's mother had a position of great importance and influence (2 Sam 14:2, 20:16; Jdt 11:18; 1 Kg 2:19 ff). The sayings reproduce traditional warnings against lust, drunkenness and oppression.

Prov 31:10–31. The virtuous wife. This famous poem forms an epilogue to the book; it may have been intended to balance the warnings against the strange woman in the prologue, emphasising wisdom's personal nature, which is also more precious than jewels (31:10, cf 8:11). A full and contented home life provides the clearest evidence of true wisdom.

Would you say that human nature has much changed since the sages wrote?

Ecclesiastes
Introduction

The writer of this penetrating book calls himself Qoheleth, a name derived from the same root as *qahal*, 'assembly'. It presumably refers to his function as head of a congregation, or 'preacher'. The author places himself pseudonymically under Solomon's patronage, in line with the common custom, but he probably lived in the fifth to fourth century. The epilogue provides some insights into his character and methods (12:9–10)—he taught in the wisdom schools, but was rather critical of their exclusivist tendencies, preferring to present his insights in proverbs all could understand. His creative honesty made him impatient with superficial ideas, or traditions not borne out by experience.

Qoheleth is often described as pessimistic in his approach, and certainly his view of life's pattern and purpose contrasts sharply with the self-assurance of Proverbs and Sirach. In place of the traditional, interlinked patterns of opposites—good and evil, righteous and wicked, wise and foolish, rich and poor, peaceful and anxious—by which the sages categorised the world of man, Qoheleth stressed life's complexity. This appears in the book's random structure; there are no clear divisions, rather the author takes up, discards, and returns to his various themes as thought follows thought. He prefers to rely on experience, and concludes that the standard theories about the purpose of life are 'vanity'—empty of significance, unreal and worthless. Life cannot be ordered and structured, it is a melange of random inconsistencies. This does not lead him to lose faith in God's providence, as he finds the common forms of escapism equally fruitless. Above all, man stands under sentence of death, and this awareness pervades all his thought. Always concrete and realistic, he can see no point in any projection of life's boundaries, rejecting this even more decisively than Job, as his whole value-system lies within the limits of man's conscious existence. Death can only be faced by concentrating on life's present moment, working to make it as fruitful and satisfying as possible.

Qoheleth is sharply critical of the schools' doctrine on retribution, but here too he takes a different tack from Job. He is not so much concerned with the extreme case, the injustice of the pious man's affliction, as with the futility of the material rewards this doctrine offers. His problem is the contrast between the determinism of events in the universe, established by God's unchanging decree, and man's inability to detect the pattern of this determination. His faith in God's freedom and power leads him to believe that everything has a purpose, but only God knows it; man must still search for wisdom to break through the surface, but all human enquiry inevitably ends in frustration.

This book shows most clearly the existence, more the acceptance, of a strong critical tradition in the wisdom schools. Proverbs and Sirach are essentially conservative, but the great themes were always subject to modification as they were examined from different points of view in search of clearer insight. Qoheleth's differences from Sirach and Proverbs on the one hand, and Wisdom on the other, indicate that the crisis in the schools was one of methodology rather than doctrine. Traditional formulations can always bear criticism; this is absolutely necessary if they are to remain valid for successive generations. While Qoheleth can only be properly understood in the context of developing political and religious insight in the wisdom schools, the perennial stimulus of his thought is a measure of the validity of his approach.

8
The wisdom of Qoheleth
Eccl 1:1–12:14

Eccl 1:2–18. Empty life

Eccl 1:2–3. Qoheleth states his theme—the whole of man's life and work, all attempts to structure his world, are doomed to frustration. He is not entirely pessimistic, but indicates that all the traditional goods—wealth, health, and happiness—so much extolled in the schools, still do not satisfy the desires of man's heart.

Eccl 1:4–11. Another basic principle: the whole world is determined, fixed in an irrevocable pattern which can never be changed or modified. The same is true for man; his life moves in a recurring rhythm and he cannot alter the pattern, as what appears to be new is always echoed in history. Human progress, the myth of man's betterment, is illusory; the wise man wearies of seeing history so often repeating itself, with men unable to learn from experience. Qoheleth challenges the optimistic, linear educational theory of the schools; study and learning do not always make a good man, knowledge is not synonymous with virtue.

Eccl 1:12–18. Qoheleth begins his treatment of the themes outlined above, speaking in the person of Solomon. He uses proverbs as a pedagogic device, first stating his own thought, then pointing it up with a proverb (cf

12:9). He has always sought to understand reality, but it is frustrating—all he can say is that man's life seems to be nothing but hard work for no return (1:13–14). God is responsible for this, man cannot hope to change it (1:15, cf 7:13). Wisdom is consequently futile; he twists a proverb the sages probably used to emphasise perseverance, stressing instead the double frustration of fruitless effort. Study cannot change the world, and the man who affects wisdom can choose folly as easily as the uneducated. The schools' heavy emphasis on sober discipline leads nowhere, but can result in arrogant thinking and rigid piety, confusing a serious approach to life with honesty and virtue.

Eccl 2:1–26. Trial of pleasure, wisdom and work

Eccl 2:1–11. Qoheleth first reacts by deliberately, almost dispassionately (2:3, 9), turning hedonist. He tries all the traditional diversions of the rich, enhances his reputation with magnificent buildings and parks, and spares no effort in his search for pleasure. He cannot deny that he enjoyed it (2:10), but at the end he has to admit that this quest too is futile. Verse 12b probably indicates the reason—he must leave it all to a successor (cf 2:18–23).

Eccl 2:12–17. Since external pleasures and possessions add nothing to the essential meaning of life, Qoheleth looks to wisdom, so much extolled in the schools. It is preferable to folly to some extent, as the wise man can anticipate events and make better choices (cf Prov 4:18–19), but eventually wise and fool share the same fate. The sages promised life for the wise and death for fools, but this promise is meaningless; immortal memory too is illusory, as all men are eventually forgotten.

Eccl 2:18–23. Work, which brought some enjoyment, is useless because he must leave the things he worked for to another, who may waste it, or not appreciate it. All his effort and struggle produces nothing lasting.

Eccl 2:24–26. Qoheleth presents his conclusion, one he repeats throughout (3:12 f, 22; 5:17 f; 8:15; 9:7–10; 11:7–10). The only way to find any happiness in life is to live it as fully as possible in the present moment, without worrying about the future, or the hidden purposes of God. Everything man has comes from God, who gives to whom he pleases. True piety consists in accepting one's measure of happiness, not being disconcerted by the temporary success of the wicked. The traditional doctrine held that the sinner's wealth would pass to the righteous (Prov 13:22, 28:8); Qoheleth leaves this too to God's judgement. He attacks any desire to dominate life; it leads to frustration, because at root it is a desire to dominate God, a repudiation of man's natural limitations.

Eccl 3:1–22.   The rhythm of life

Eccl 3:1–13. Qoheleth continues his meditation on life with his famous poem on times (3:1–9). He believes that all the events of a man's life are predetermined, and that true discernment consists in recognising the rhythm of human relations. He uses the method of contrasting opposites, symbolically expressing at once the inherent determinism of events as well as their apparent randomness. Only God knows the whole extent of the world's interaction; man can appreciate it in theory but cannot always discern the pattern in practice, because God has put eternity, 'the timeless', into his heart (3:10–11). Man yearns for absolutes, so he can miss the limits and outline of the pattern God sets up. Since man's life is bound by these restrictions, some good and some hurtful, the only solution is to make the most of the moments of real enjoyment, to see them as a gift from God and a share in the harmony of creation. Contentment lies in accepting that life cannot be manipulated, that good and ill come to all, and are willed by God. This is not amorphous escapism, for Qoheleth is always careful to stress the value of work, but the way to maturity (3:12–13). The reference to gathering stones (3:5) is probably a euphemism for sexual relations, as indicated by the parallelism.

Eccl 3:14–22. The mystery of God's dominion

God, as well as the world, is determined; he always acts consistently, he cannot change his own patterns (cf Ps 33:11; Sir 18:6, 42:41). This poses a problem for the notion of his providence; God affects men's lives mysteriously, uncertainty results in fear (3:14–15). Experience shows that there is no absolute justice in human affairs; the traditional explanations of eventual retribution, and the testing of the just, depend on faith rather than experience (3:16–18). God perhaps allows injustice to let man see his own limitations, his cruel unthinking side that is also part of nature's legacy. Man and beast at times seem much the same, certainly both are subject to death. Their nature is not the same but their eventual end may be—no one knows (3:19–21). Qoheleth gives the same advice—only the present has real value—the tradition of a future judgement is useless for man cannot see into the future (3:22).

1. How much power does man have to change himself?
2. Why do we tend to resist the fact that our life is in many respects determined by events beyond our control?

3. Is the 'timeless' in man's heart any indication of future life?

Eccl 4:1–16. Man's injustice to man

Qoheleth has already mentioned this problem (3:16); he now discusses it in greater detail.

Eccl 4:1–3. Power alone decides a man's fate; there is no justice or retribution. Qoheleth feels this anomaly deeply; so much so that he considers the dead or the unborn fortunate, a measure of his distress in view of the fact that death for him is the ultimate loss.

Eccl 4:4–6. Injustice results from man's need to bolster his self-importance, to dominate others, as a measure of his self-esteem. The schools considered laziness the supreme folly (Prov 6:9–11; cf the bitter contempt of Prov 26:13; Sir 22), extolling diligence (Prov 6:11, 10:4 f, 12:27); Qoheleth points out the other side, over-emphasis on effort does not always bring peace.

Eccl 4:7–12. In fact, it may cut a man off from others. The man who concentrates on his work to the exclusion of all else may satisfy some of his own emotional needs, but he is likely to end up frustrated and lonely, without family or friends. Unable to work productively with others, he buries himself in his work; without it he is lost, but he does not realise he is lost anyway (4:7–8). Qoheleth opts for combining work with real human interaction; this gives real satisfaction (4:9–12).

Eccl 4:13–16. A man may work hard for social success, and Qoheleth gives a convincing portrait of a poor young man who concentrates everything on moving up the ladder of power and influence. When he reaches the

summit, he finds nobody loves him; he has nobody to
share his success with. He is even isolated from advice,
and would have been better off if he had remained poor.
Respect for his memory becomes more precious to him,
but he has left it too late.

Eccl 5:1–7. True worship

A set of maxims about the pious Israelite's religious
duties, applying wisdom's traditional concern for careful
speech. The wisdom writers, as one would expect from
the sting they pack into proverbs, were extremely conscious of the power of language; they constantly stress
the considered and cautious use of words. Unreflec-
tive speech not only betrays a shallow mind, but may
cause untold damage out of all proportion to its own
worth.

When a man goes to the temple, he does better just to
listen than to spend time in wordy prayers; Qoheleth
warns against any tendency to browbeat God in prayer,
as this only indicates lack of real faith and confidence (cf
Prov 10:19). Respect for God demands that once a vow
is made it be promptly kept; he warns against making it
hastily (Prov 20:25; Sir 18:22 ff). A man can be held
responsible for inadvertent sins; it is no use to plead a
slip of the tongue to the angel who informs God of man's
deeds (Num 15, 22 ff; Tob 12:12). He finishes with a
second summary proverb (5:7); a large vocabulary does
not always indicate intelligence, real reverence is better
than beautiful prayers (cf Sir 34:15).

Eccl 5:8–6:6. The problems of money

Eccl 5:8–9. Anger at social injustice usually meets these
perennial excuses, as responsibility is shifted up the chain

into oblivion, and officials plead the demands of the common good.

Eccl 5:10–12. Two proverbs indicate the basic reason. The rich never want to share but only to increase their wealth indefinitely, they can never have enough. But they must also protect it from the inevitable parasites, as greed feeds on greed. The man who has sufficient for his needs is free of care; ulcers and isolation reward the rich.

Eccl 5:14–17. A poor businessman may lose all and have nothing to leave to his heir; he ends up as poor as he began. In general, material things are all useless as they do not last through death, the end of all man's striving, and final proof that this too is pointless.

Eccl 5:18–20. The only reasonable thing to do is to concentrate on simple pleasures, live and work fully and contentedly with what God gives. God's gift is not so much the possession of wealth and comfort, as the ability to live contentedly in the midst of prosperity. The one thing he warns against is that devouring dissatisfaction that makes a man wretched within, no matter how rich he is. Qoheleth is obviously impatient with the limited 'days of his life'; this he can only sublimate by his accepting life's real benefits as God's gift (5:20).

Eccl 6:1–6. A meditation on the confines of human existence. In many ways the stillborn infant is better off than the successful and respected man, a thought which would have been 'offensive to pious ears' for many of Qoheleth's audience. The rich man must leave all behind, to someone else; he may not even be buried, the ultimate disgrace. He parodies patriarchal fecundity and old age (6:3, 6) to point out that even the covenant promises have their limits. The stillborn child at least does not know the thwarting of its hope or the fear of failure; without any prior pain it too finds rest in *she'ol*'s darkness.

1. Is ambition irreconcilable with religion?

2. Is Qoheleth too sceptical of any attempt to make changes by action?

Eccl 6:7–12. What use is wisdom?

Man's need for survival is the only reason why he has to work; but this is never enough, he always wants to understand his life and so can never find peace. The wise man may be no better off than the fool, or the poor man whose sole concern is to keep up appearances. He would do better just to accept things as they seem (6:9), for he cannot change their nature, thus disputing with God (6:10). The more he learns, the less he knows; he may attempt to master the world with words, but this only obscures what it is meant to clarify, and life's purpose can be lost in play-acting. The problem is basically insoluble, as the world remains immune from man's comprehension.

Eccl 7:1–12. Some practical benefits of wisdom

A group of comparison-sayings, with added commentary, perhaps intended to counterbalance any wrong impressions from earlier statements. He uses alliteration frequently—7:1 reads *tov shem mishshemen tov*—a good name at the end of life is better than a life just beginning (cf 6: 3–5). Sorrow is closer to the reality of life than frivolity (7:3–4, cf 3:12–13, 8:15); correction is better than having fun with the boys, as thorns crackle loudly but give little heat (7:5–6). Even the wise can be corrupted, so it is better to look for results than listen to proud predictions (7:7–8). Resentful living in the past is useless, for it changes nothing (7:9–10, cf 1:10–11). The author is unimpressed by the traditional high regard for wealth and wisdom; but accepts that both do have some practical value, wisdom especially helping to prolong and enhance life.

Eccl 7:13–8:1. The paradox of life

Eccl 7:13–14. Man cannot change the way things are (cf 1:15); God sends both good and evil, and man should enjoy the good and accept the rest. Evil cannot be explained away, it is sent by God to remind man that he does not control his fate.

Eccl 7:15–18. Experience contradicts the principle of strict retribution. Both those who try to ensure their fate by being totally righteous, and those who opt for success by unjust means, face eventual frustration. A man should consider both alternatives carefully—Qoheleth himself advocates a reverent acceptance of God's will (cf 3:14–15).

Eccl 7:19–22. Some further elaborations on the above. Wisdom ranks above political power (9:16, cf Prov 21:22); and no man is completely virtuous (cf 7:16). The temptation to listen to a telltale or repress criticism comes from the desire to be always in the right.

Eccl 7:23–25. Qoheleth sought wisdom, like all the great teachers; ultimately he had to acknowledge it was beyond him (cf Job 28; Sir 1:5–7). All he could find was a measure of discernment, the difference between wisdom and folly.

Eccl 7:26–29. This is especially clear in the case of the seductress, as her devious enticements provide a living standard for discernment. Qoheleth is not so much concerned with giving his pupils the usual warning against such women (cf Prov 2:16–19; Sir 9:1–9); but tries to understand the reason for this situation. He is somewhat misogynistic (not completely so, cf 9:9), a common enough tendency among thinkers, who tend to blame women for emotionally confusing clear thought. However honesty compels him to admit that pretence and dissimulation are common to all, man and woman alike.

Eccl 8:1. A saying in praise of wisdom and the wise.

Eccl 8:2–15. Political problems

Eccl 8:2–4. The king must always be obeyed, for his authority is sacred, consecrated by oath; his power cannot be gainsaid.

Eccl 8:5–9. 8:5 is a proverb which the author wants to examine. Is it always right to obey, will everything work out in the end? Qoheleth agrees that every situation has its own determined dynamic, but this is usually not obvious to man; death, war, and sin establish absolute limits beyond his control. Obedience does not remove oppression.

Eccl 8:10–15. This leads him again to the problem of retribution. The Hebrew text of 8:10 reads: 'And this I saw; wicked men buried, who entered and left the holy place; and those who acted rightly were not remembered in the city'. The text is uncertain, it presumably refers in some way to the anomaly of human respect for the powerful. Another problem comes from the fact that the wicked are not swiftly punished, so men desire to emulate them. In spite of appearances, Qoheleth affirms his faith in eventual retribution, taking refuge in the principle almost for its own sake; fear of God is its own reward, the ultimate paradox that is so utterly true (8:12–13). He restates the paradox, offering the same advice as before; it can only be resolved by avoiding extremes and finding enjoyment in what God gives.

Eccl 8:16–9:10. Love and hatred

Eccl 8:16–17. Traditional wisdom attempted to define life by its categories of opposites; Qoheleth considers them rather as paradox, pointing out that the wise man's task, seeking to discover and delimit the work of God, is always doomed to fail.

Eccl 9:1–6. God's supreme power rules every man's life but no one can judge whether God loves or hates him simply by what happens to him. All men must eventually die, and the only advantage the living have is that they at least know this. Life, however, is better than death, for the dead know nothing, can feel nothing.

Eccl 9:7–10. In view of 9:5, the best thing to do is live and love with as much enjoyment as possible in the days remaining; there is nothing wrong in this, as God has established it.

Eccl 9:11–16. Destiny and chance

Eccl 9:11–12. Man expects due rewards for virtue and skill, but everything has its appointed time, which he does not know (3:1–12). Everything appears to him to be ruled by chance; he considers himself the victim of bad luck, when virtue's hope is unexpectedly thwarted.

Eccl 9:13–16. This applies even to wisdom, as he illustrates with a parable. The sages rated wisdom above power (Prov 21:22), but Qoheleth observes that it is not always effective. He tells of a man whose wisdom saved a city; the incident impressed him, but evidently not the citizens. Wisdom does not always bring men to see the light.

1. Must virtue always be rewarded?

2. Is Qoheleth's advice simply to enjoy life without any thought of the consequences?

Eccl 9:17–11:8. Miscellaneous proverbs

Eccl 9:17–10:1. Three comparisons between wisdom and folly introduce this wisdom lesson. Wisdom is powerful; but so is folly, often out of all proportion to its intrinsic worth, as one mistake can undo much good work.

Eccl 10:2–3. The right hand is the hand of blessing; for 10:3 cf Prov 13:16.

Eccl 10:4. Advice to lie low when in disfavour (Prov 14:17).

Eccl 10:5–7. More of life's anomalies (Prov 19:10).

Eccl 10:8–11. Four one-liners illustrating that what man works for may not always help him; the first saying was a favourite of the sages (Ps 7:15; Prov 26:27; Sir 27:26–27). Qoheleth adds his own comments (10:10–11); even the wise man can make life harder for himself.

Eccl 10:12–15. Traditional sayings on foolish speech, to which Qoheleth adds his own comment on the folly of trying to know the future (10:14).

Eccl 10:16–20. Two sayings contrast the fate of the lands whose rulers are either self-indulgent or sober (10:16–17). He adds his own comments on 10:16; laziness leads to neglect of their land's basic needs (10:18), their complaisant excuses are insufficient (10:19). But one should be careful not to complain too loudly, as walls have ears (10:20).

Eccl 11:1–8. The sage's practical advice: take some chances (11:1), but do not put all your eggs in one basket (11:2). No one knows what may happen as everything is determined, but there is no profit in being idle (11:3–4). God's ways are mysterious, but he does allow some things to prosper; even though it must all end, life has many compensations (11:5–8).

Eccl 11:9–12:8. Youth and age

Eccl 11:9–12:1. The sages usually emphasised discipline, sobriety and restraint to curb impetuous youth; Qoheleth tells the young man to enjoy his youth to the utmost, when few avenues have been closed off and all is still promise. The reminder of eventual judgement is perhaps added later (11:9, cf 12:14); Qoheleth himself knows disillusionment is inevitable.

Eccl 12:1–8. This graphic description of the gradual failing of his hold on life illustrates Qoheleth's keen sense of loss, the contrast between the dimming of his own activity and perception and the burgeoning life around him. Men mourn the old before they are dead (12:5), and this adds to the pain. Eventually life stops; man's body turns to dust and his spirit returns to God. No man can escape this final limitation.

Eccl 12:9–14. Epilogue

Eccl 12:9–11. Written by one of his disciples, this short passage shows the affection they had for their shepherd (12:11). He was a genuine teacher; original, yet concerned to present his thought in an acceptable fashion, always honest with himself.

Eccl 12:12–14. These verses may perhaps be intended to correct any misapprehensions. Not many can be as independent in their thinking as he (cf Jas 3:1), and the traditional doctrine remains valid; reverence for God's law must be paramount, as everything is subject to his judgement—something Qoheleth believed (3:17) but maintained could never be demonstrated (9:1–3).

How courageous is the stoic?

Sirach (Ecclesiasticus)
Introduction

Jesus ben Eleazar ben Sira, a well-educated, much-travelled, upper-middle class scholar, lived in Jerusalem around the beginning of the second century BC, when the Palestinian Jews were beginning to feel the effects of the profound cultural transformation set in motion by Alexander. Palestine's Seleucid overlords, searching for new sources of revenue after massive defeats at the hands of the Romans, plundered the temple treasury, and tried to submerge any sense of national identity by imposing the Greek language and cultural system (2 Mac 3–5; 1 Mac 1:11–15). This process of deliberate hellenisation was most abhorrent to pious Jews, whose struggle for national identity formed the core of their religious history, and who could never accept a foreign theocracy as could the syncretistic pagan religions. Eventually, in the reign of Antiochus Epiphanes, the Seleucid campaign led to open revolt under the Maccabees (1 Mac 1; 4:5–10). At the time Sirach wrote his book, the situation had not reached this extreme; he was simply concerned to restate Israel's own traditions and piety by collecting an anthology of traditional wisdom, concluding with a hymn in praise of the fathers, to demonstrate the inherent superiority of Israel's religious and ethical tradition.

While Sirach's purpose was, in the Palestinian situation, similar to that of the author of the Wisdom of

Solomon, his methods were those of the classic wisdom teacher. He presents a series of extended wisdom-lessons, similar to those found in the prologue to Proverbs, linked by catchwords, mots-crochets and thematic affinity; but he goes far beyond Proverbs in his appreciation of the demands of true worship, and his equiparation of wisdom with the law. Wisdom is God's gift to Israel, it has its true home in Jerusalem.

The book was translated into Greek in Alexandria by ben Sira's grandson sometime after his arrival in Egypt in the thirty-eighth year of Ptolemy Euergetes VII (132 BC) (whence the name Sirach—the final 'chi' was possibly a spelling convention not meant to be pronounced, or a transliteration for the Hebrew letter *he*), for the education and edification of Jew and Greek in the diaspora. Until the discovery of some Hebrew manuscripts in the Cairo *genizah* (a walled-off portion of the synagogue where manuscripts containing the divine name were placed after they became worn or otherwise unusable), the work was known only in translation. Since that time, further MSS have been found at Qumran, and at the present time approximately two-thirds of the book is extant in Hebrew.

The Latin title *Ecclesiasticus* presumably refers either to the book's extensive use in the christian church, especially in the liturgy, where it is the most frequently quoted work after the psalms, or to the dispute about its canonicity, which was not definitively settled until the council of Trent. The Hebrew canon was defined at the council of Jamnia in 100 AD; and the dominant pharisaic party presumably excluded Ben Sira because of its rejection of any notion of resurrection or life after death, and lack of interest in messianism, two characteristics of the later priestly aristocratic sadducees, of which Ben Sira was a forerunner.

9

Life with wisdom
Sir 1:1–16:23

Prologue

For an active and penetrating tradition, the wisdom
movement produced relatively few works, and the grandson of Jesus ben Sira hints at some dissatisfaction with
scholarship for its own sake in his introduction. When he
came to Egypt and found that intense scholarly activity
and contact with the question raised by the philosophers
had already resulted in the translation of many of the
books of the Hebrew scriptures, he determined to add to
them the work of his grandfather, which he allies with
the 'other writings', the first mention of the traditional
threefold division. Ben Sira had studied the scriptures
thoroughly, and his work shares in their authority; in
the grandson's opinion it deserves to rank in this last
section, which was evidently not as well defined as the
law and the prophets. He hopes thus to bring this
masterly summary of Israel's traditions to a wider
audience, though he is aware of the difficulties facing
all translators. The wheel has now turned full circle,
as wisdom's internationalism, as well as assimilating
the insights of Egyptian and Greek thinkers, now
concentrates on the attempt to bring its own religious
and human values into fruitful contact with other
cultures.

Sir 1:1–30. The praise of wisdom

Sir 1:1–10. God is the source of all wisdom; she was his agent in creating the pattern of the world (Prov 8:22–31). God alone possesses wisdom, but he has given her to men to some extent, to those who have come to trust and love him.

Sir 1:11–20. Two short poems describe the basic dispositions for acquiring wisdom. The 'fear of the Lord', wholehearted reverence and respect for God, produces a joyous and full life (1:11–13); it is the beginning (1:14, 20) and end (1:16, 18) of wisdom (cf Prov 1:7).

Sir 1:22–30. The concrete demands of 'fear of the Lord' include patient endurance, keeping the commandments, and absolute honesty, the elements of covenant fidelity.

Sir 2:1–18. Endurance

This chapter comments on the first necessary condition, that of patient endurance in the testing-time (1:22–25).

Sir 2:1–6. A standard introductory warning to those who had made an initial commitment to 'serve the Lord', that its working out would involve trial and testing. It reaches back to Israel's desert experience (Ex 16:4, Deut 8:2–5), and was applied especially to leaders and teachers in the troubled period under Seleucid rule (cf Jdt 8:25–27; Wis 2:10–20). A similar pattern recurs in the new testament (cf Jas 1:2–4; 1 Pet 1:6–7; Rev 2:10).

Sir 2:7–18. Four three-line stanzas comment on the admonition, emphasising the need for faith and hope (2:7–9) and the pattern of promise and reward for endurance in Israel's history (2:10). The three-fold woe-oracle curses the apostates who have turned back from commitment in time of trial (2:12–14, cf Lk 6:24–25), while the final stanza equates 'fear of the Lord' with the love of God, expressed in unselfish devotion to the law (2:14–15, cf Jn 14:15). 2:11, 18 are short antiphonal responses possibly recited by the pupils; the former is a credal summary and the latter a prayer (cf 2 Sam 24:14).

Sir 3:1–4:19. The laws of God

Sir 3:1–16. A commentary on the fourth commandment (Ex 20:12), developing the second precondition (1:26–27). Fidelity to this commandment also atones for sins (3:3, 14–15).

Sir 3:17–28. Humility binds the community together (1 Pet 5:5), obtains the promise (Prov. 3:34; Mt 20:26–28) and finds favour with God (Jas 4:6). It is the way to wisdom; Sirach attacks the mystery religions and philosophical cults which stressed esoteric knowledge as the key to salvation, a tendency also attacked by Paul (1 Cor 1–3). Some Jews had been too readily influenced by the superficial attractions of hellenistic sophistry; Sirach is not anti-intellectual, simply against that kind of intellectual pride that is too sure of itself.

Sir 3:29–4:10. True wisdom does not despise the poor but cares for them; this is the sign of genuine humility, and contrasts traditional Jewish concern with the Greek idea which tended to find fault in poverty. Almsgiving, like reverence for parents, atones for sin (Tob 4:10; Dan 4:27).

Sir 4:11–19. This returns to the theme of 2:1–18, describing wisdom's testing of her disciple. 4:11 states the general principle, 4:12–16 outlines wisdom's benefits in covenant terms, and 4:17–19 describes the moment of initial decision. The chiastic structure of the Greek in the latter section emphasises the central purpose of this process, the establishment of wisdom's trust in the committed disciple.

Sir 4:20–6:4. Sincerity

Sir 4:20–31. The third covenant-prerequisite (1:28–30) is complete sincerity and honesty in commitment. The hellenisers used every possible method to induce the Jews to change their life-style; some of the more susceptible had begun to adopt a double standard. The author warns against hiding one's faith when challenged because of human respect.

Sir 5:1–10. Desire for wealth and influence was the cause of this dissembling. As the Seleucid rulers became embroiled in Jewish politics and the high priesthood was bargained for among rival factions, true piety and wisdom declined. Sirach warns against presumption (cf Wis 2:11; Eccl 8:11–14), and disparaging over-confidence in God's eventual mercy, after the deals have been made.

Sir 5:11–6:4. Sirach returns to the theme of sincerity, concentrating especially on the advantages of steadfast consistency. He advises the student to be deliberate, then gives two negative examples: warning against slander (5:14–6:1) and haughty bad temper (6:2–4).

Sir 6:5–17. Friendship

The thought of the man isolated through pride (6:2–4) leads Sirach to consider the benefits of genuine friendship. Implicitly, he shows that a true relationship with God is also one of friendship, for the process of making friends follows the same lines. Friendship comes slowly and is proved in trial, as the disadvantages of fairweather friends (6:8–10, 11–13) are set against the benefits a faithful friend brings (6:14–16). True piety is the best criterion; a man who is faithful to God will make a faithful friend (6:17).

Sir 6:18–37. The search for wisdom

Three strophes of six, nine and six lines comprise an instruction on the way to get wisdom, using the metaphors of farming, the yoke, and instruction from elders.

Sir 6:18–22. Another form of the initial warning that the search for wisdom involves trial. The quest never ceases throughout life; like farming, it is a process of constant renewal, requiring perseverance in making constantly crucial decisions. 6:22 is a pun on the Hebrew word *musar*, which means 'wisdom', 'discipline' or, in a different form, 'withdrawn'.

Sir 6:23–31. The invitation to accept wisdom's yoke and the bonds of her discipline remind us of the words of Christ (Mt 11:29–30).

Sir 6:32–37. Application and willingness to listen are essential; also study of the law opens the way to God's gift of wisdom, granting man's initial desire.

Sir 7:1–9:16. Relations with others

A series of prohibitions, commenting on the general command in 7:1–2.

Sir 7:1–17. The author warns against becoming embroiled in the civil service, which in the Seleucid courts had led many Jews to compromise their religious principles.

Sir 7:18–36. Sirach turns his attention to man's more personal relations in his family, among his friends and in his social life. Reverence for priests is unusual in wisdom writings, as is the mention of honouring the dead, especially as Sirach rejects any notion of life after death.

Sir 8:1–19. Respect for all ages balances prudence in dealing with the powerful, but for the sage self-interest is not the same as selfishness, rather it is an awareness of the facts of life combined with a search for genuine values.

Sir 9:1–9. Sirach comments on his opening maxim in the standard wisdom warning against the wrong kinds of sexual relationships. Jealousy and lack of understanding between husband and wife may lead either to seek outside consolation, to the ultimate destruction of both.

Sir 9:10–16. Friends come gradually, and the man of discernment seeks out good men with whom he can build genuine friendship.

Sir 9:17–11:28. Advice for the eminent

Sir 10:1–5. Wise rulers, who reverence the Lord, will contribute to the well-being of all, because they carry out the designs of God, and find their true reward and honour in serving him.

Sir 10:6–18. The root of bad government is pride; since it goes against God's plan, God will eventually punish the proud and restore the humble. Sirach looks to the eventual destruction of the arrogant Seleucids (cf Dan 4:19–33).

Sir 10:19–11:6. Man earns honour or disgrace, and it is fear of the Lord that makes the difference. All outward signs of eminence are worthless without this.

Sir 11:7–28. Sirach's caution about overvaluing wealth (10:27) leads him to consider the problem of retribution, and the value of work and ambition (cf Eccl 2:18–23). Three transitional verses invite the reader to reflect on what he is about to say (11:7–9); then comes the general admonition (11:10), reinforced by the contrasting fate of the 'tortoise and hare' (11:11–13). Everything is subject to the Lord's disposition (11:14–19, cf Prov 16:1–9, Lk 12:16–21); the wise man will stick to his agreement with God and not be disconcerted by the apparent prosperity of the wicked.

Sir 11:29–14:2. On choosing friends and associates

Sir 11:29–34. Sirach warns against letting a stranger into one's home, as he may be looking to steal, or to take advantage of generosity; he is perhaps thinking of a non-Israelite, who would have none of the moral compunction of the pious Jew.

Sir 12:1–18. Good deeds should be rewarded, and not necessarily in heaven. Good can only be done to the good, as the just man should share in God's desire for retribution, an attitude which will be finally overturned only in the new testament (Mt 5:43–47). In line with this, a man should never trust his enemy even if he appears to relent, for the sage knows he will regret it eventually.

Sir 13:1–14:2. Sirach warns against overmuch association with the rich; the hanger-on is ripe for exploitation.

The rich man's flattery springs from contempt, so a wise man will associate with his equals, as rich and poor do not mix well. The rich always have helpers, the poor are despised for their poverty. Sirach emphasises that it is the interior attitude, not wealth or poverty itself, that makes the difference, and warns against judging by appearances as the wise and good man may not always seem to be happy or prosperous.

Sir 14:3–19. Material enjoyment

Sirach's advice resembles that given by Qoheleth (cf Eccl 5:10–20). The miser does not enjoy his wealth, even his generosity is selfish; eventually he must lose all his possessions, as he has already lost all chance of friendship. Every man must die, so he should enjoy what he has while he has it, sharing with God and man alike.

Sir 14:20–16:23. A wisdom lesson

This contrasts the wise man's attitude with the thinking of the misguided fool.

Sir 14:20–15:8. The beatitude describes the man who hears wisdom's call (Prov 8:32–35; Wis 6:12–16) and importunes her constantly (14:20–27). Because he fears the Lord and keeps the law she rewards him with genuine joy and happiness, again described in traditional terms (cf Prov 9:5; Wis 6:16; 8:2, 10–16).

Sir 15:9–10. Only the just man can offer fitting praise to God.

Sir 15:11–20. Sirach would not accept Qoheleth's determinism or Greek fatalism; man is responsible for his choices and actions. God's power is not an excuse for sin; nor does he permit it (cf Jas 1:13–14).

Sir 16:1–23. In fact, God punishes sin. For the pious Jew, immortality came through one's children; many sons both signified God's blessing and ensured a lasting memory. But if a man's sons deserted the fear of the Lord they brought no benefit and would not escape punishment (cf Ez 18:10–13, 20). A large family is no use of itself; one wise man is worth more than many wicked, since as a true spiritual father he brings many to wisdom and understanding.

Sirach illustrates the principle from Israel's history (16:5–10). Fire destroyed the rebellious Israelites, and water the over-confident giants of old (Gen 6:1–7). Sodom and Gomorrah perished in their pride (Gen 19:1–29); the Canaanite tribes were dispossessed, and many of the more fractious Israelites never reached the promised land but died in the desert (Ex 12:37; Num 11:21). God's punishment is as sure as his mercy is great, and the unrepentant sinner will certainly be punished, as Sirach builds on Ezekiel's doctrine of individual retribution (Ez 33:10–20; Job 34:11).

The wicked man thinks he can go unnoticed by God, or like Adam and Cain he tries to hide (Gen 3:10, 4:9; cf Ps 139:7–12) for God's justice is not always apparent, and the covenant, the time of final appointment of the promise, seems far in the future (cf 14:12). 16:18–20a is a parenthetical reminder of the signs of God's power, which the foolish neglect.

1. In what sense is it true to say that life is 'full of trials'?
2. How does Sirach's attitude towards the poor and dispossessed appear in the light of the gospels?

*3. 'Before a man are life and death, and whichever he
chooses will be given to him' (15 : 17). In the light of Sirach's
this-worldly eschatology, what does this statement have to offer to
our conceptions of retribution?*

10

In praise of creation
Sir 16:24–23:27

Because it resembles the opening chapter in its form of
address and praise of creation, many commentators consider that 16:24–17:20 begins a second major section of
the book; it is however possible that it is another introductory discourse following on 16:18–20 and preparing
for the call to repentance (17:21–18:14).

Sir 16:24–17:20. Creation

The usual sapiential introduction (16:24–25) begins a
meditation on creation. Sirach describes the separation
of the elements (Gen 1:3–13) and the constant order of
the stars which, unlike man, never disobey God (Gen 1
14–19). All living things come from God, though they do
not last forever (cf Gen 3:19; Ps 104:29).

Man too must die (Eccl 3:20), even though by God's
gift he rules the rest of creation (Ps 8:5; Gen 1:28) and
shares in God's power. In Genesis, man only gained discernment, the knowledge of good and evil, after the fall;
Sirach gives this a positive sense, the capacity to praise
and acknowledge God. Creation and history both witness
to God's power (17:8–10); Sirach sees the Sinai covenant as the natural continuation of God's creation. The
commandments are summed up in the dual avoidance of
evil and positive concern for one's neighbour. Israel is

the Lord's portion, a necessary reminder in this time of oppression; God's provident concern watches over her always, and he scrutinises those who neglect her covenant and traditions.

Sir 17:21–18:14. God's mercy

The generous will receive their reward eventually, but God is also concerned for those who are tempted to abandon the covenant, who lack endurance in the test-ing-time. If they repent and return they will find forgive-ness. Sirach addresses the faint-hearted who had shown themselves most susceptible to the pervading pressures of hellenism, bidding them reject any compromise in case they be punished by premature death. He outlines the process of repentance; first the initial decision, followed by prayer, then gradual withdrawal from evil practices (17:25, cf 1 Cor 8:9; Rom 9:32).

Sirach equates God's power and mercy; God alone is wholly just for he has created everything. Qoheleth and Job both saw God's justice as based on his power (Job 9:1–12, 12:13–25; Eccl 9:1 f); Sirach instead compares their range. 18:4–6 resembles Eccl 3:14–15, but Sirach rather sides with Job—man's search is fruitless because of God's greatness. God does recognise man's weakness and brief life-span (Ps 8:4; Job 7:17–18); because of this he shows mercy, gently correcting all men and leading them to repentance (Wis 11:21–12:2). Sirach moderates the common view that he corrected only the Israelites and destroyed their enemies (2 Mac 6:12–17).

Sir 18:15–23:27. Practical advice for avoiding sin

Sir 18:15–29. Prudence and foresight provide the best protection. 18:15–18 comments on human generosity

(18:13); cold charity cannot compare with genuine concern. 18:19–26 offers general counsels on proper caution;
the man who vows rashly tests the Lord because he himself fails in the testing-time between promise and fulfilment (18:23, cf Prov 20:25; Eccl 5:4–6). The wise man
is especially wary in troubled times, when pressured to
turn from God; he also has a responsibility to share his
wisdom in this situation (Dan 11:33).

Sir 18:30–19:3. Control of sensuality was prized by
Greek as well as Jew; Sirach reminds his hearers that unbridled pleasure-seeking ends in untimely and unpleas-
ant death (19:3).

Sir 19:4–17. Control of the tongue was a constant
concern of the sages. Sirach repeats previous admoni-
tions, ending with the warning against gossip, on which
he wants to expand (18:6). Tale-bearing always results
in estrangement, as it disrupts the fabric of society; only
fools need the superficial attention it brings. Sirach advises making a direct approach in any dispute; whether
something is true or not, this brings better results and the
judgement can safely be left to God.

Sir 19:20–30. The mention of the law links into a discussion of the qualities of true wisdom. Sirach does not so
much equate wisdom with fear of the Lord and observance of law, as insist that true wisdom must include these.
He attacks sophistry, devious legalism, hypocrisy, and
the confusion of wisdom with intelligence, all likely results of accepting hellenistic values. The sages considered
genuine wisdom to be manifested in a man's manner and
appearance (cf Eccl 8:1).

Sir 20:1–31. Sirach meditates on the proper times for
speech, the rhythm of relationships of which the wise

man is aware but the fool always misses. He indicates the complex and subtle nature of this rhythm by his use of paradox, antithesis and contrasting sayings. Human respect and lies bring eventual shame, but the wise man finds honour and advancement. He must however be careful of the wrong kind of honours, intended to keep him quiet (Prov 21:14); the wise man has an obligation to speak out against impiety and injustice (Wis 2:12–14).

Sir 21:1–10. If a man should sin, he must repent and pray (17:25–26). Sin is essentially destructive because it has no solid foundation and ends in certain retribution. The sinner deceives only himself, whereas the sensible man is aware of his faults (21:7).

Sir 21:11–22:18. Various situations and sayings contrast the wise man and the fool. Again, wisdom is the perfection of fear of the Lord and the keeping of law, which enables a man to control his evil impulses, a reference presumably to the dichotomous concept of man's dual tendencies developed by the rabbis and used by Paul. Sirach insists again on will-power (cf 15:14–17). Intelligence is necessary to be wise, but some intelligent men, who question too much, may bitterly reject wisdom. 21:13–28 contrast the wise and the foolish; 21:19 is misplaced, and should come immediately before or after 21:21. Folly is betrayed in boorish conduct (21:22–24); the fool talks unthinkingly while the sage reflects beforehand. Cursing and slander betray wickedness rather than remove it (21:27–28).

The sages were especially contemptuous of laziness (cf Prov 26:13–16); and also considered unruly or irreligious children a reflexion on their parents, and the only remedy severe discipline (cf Prov 13:24, 19:18, 22:15). This would always be effective, but verbal rebuke could easily backfire. The sages were scarcely evangelistic; Sirach counsels against wasting time trying to teach those who do not want to accept wisdom as it is futile and frustrating; one can only weep for them, knowing that their whole life is at stake.

Wisdom's importance consists in the fact that it supports a man in time of crisis, whereas a fool has nothing to fall back on, so lacks endurance (cf 2:1–14).

Sir 22:19–26. The need for constancy in one's relation with God leads Sirach again to the parallel situation of human friendship. Constancy is necessary here too, but while thoughtless remarks may damage a friendship, this can be repaired; like one's relation with God, it is only deliberate offence that ruins all chance of reconciliation. Friends made in misfortune are usually more genuine than those made in prosperity (cf 6:5–17); the poor were considered sinners according to the standard theory of retribution, but Sirach knows this is not always true. If a poor man is virtuous he should be befriended then, as his reward will surely come and by then the friendship is already soundly based.

Sir 22:27–23:27. Sirach prays for help in avoiding sins of speech and thought, in the latter case especially the desires of the flesh. 22:27–23:6 introduces the section in parallel form, 22:27 asking for protection against sins of the tongue followed by a prayer (23:1) and 23:2–3 asking for help against lustful desires, with the prayer in 23:4–6. Sirach, who has stressed man's freedom, is also aware of the strength of desire and the tongue's susceptibility for sin, against which man needs God's help.

Sir 23:7–15. Sirach warns against swearing, and rash oath-taking, which can be doubly dangerous if the oath is taken lightly and not carried out, because it offends

both God and man. Blasphemy is the worst of sins (23:
12), and vulgarity and coarseness alienates a man from
any worthwhile friends. Bad language and careless speech
indicate immaturity.

Sir 23:16–26. The sins of the flesh are introduced by a
numerical proverb, stressing the third type. 23:16 in the
Greek text castigates solitary sins, and 23:17 fornication,
of its nature indiscriminate. 23:18–26 concentrates on
adultery, the most serious of all, since it offends God's
law as well as disrupting social order. Essentially deceit-
ful, it cannot escape God's sanctions, and will eventually
be punished. Public scourging, rather than death (Lev
20:10), was the usual punishment at this time (23:21,
24). The adulteress, besides scourging, was usually punished by divorce and expulsion from the community,
who could also pass judgement on the legitimacy of her
children.

Sir 23:27. A solemn conclusion to the second section,
stressing the twin pillars of reverence for God and respect
for the law.

*1. Is it true that chastising and discipline are wisdom at all
times?*

*2. Do we take carelessness in speech with sufficient serious-
ness?*

11

In praise of wisdom and of the fathers
Sir 24:1–51:30

Sir 24:1–34. The famous hymn to wisdom introduces this section; coming at the centre of the book, it highlights with deliberate emphasis the development and depth of late wisdom speculation. Wisdom is personified (Prov 8:22; Bar 3:9 ff; Job 28), emanating from God like the spirit at creation (24:3, cf Gen 1:2) yet distinct from him. She pervades all of creation but finds her home in Israel, specifically in the Jerusalem temple. She invites all men to search for her, especially those Jews who were attracted by hellenism, for she offers unending delight. The sage then offers further comment on wisdom's discourse (24:23–29). Wisdom was always considered mysterious, offering herself to men but only attainable to a limited extent through study and reflexion; but Sirach identifies her with the torah. He goes beyond all previous doctrine; wisdom is now recognisable and concrete, equated with fulfilment of the law. The image of the great rivers of the east (24:27 is a mistranslation from the Hebrew, and should read 'Nile' for 'light') as well as the rivers of paradise, coupled with the successive stages of the harvest, symbolically indicates wisdom's spread and development from the first man, through the ancient civilisations, to Israel. The sage likens himself to an irrigation conduit, drawing from this immense source of growth-bringing water, gradually overflowing to spread wisdom's influence far and wide (24:30–34).

Sir 25:1–26:18. A series of numerical proverbs, giving particular advice on human relationships. 25:1–2 introduces the section with a numerical antithesis; the usual climactic effect is lacking, but the last lines emphasise the importance of the marriage relationship on which Sirach expands later. 25:3–6 comments on 25:2; wisdom normally becomes old age, as long as it has been earned by proper discipline (Prov 16:31, cf Wis 4:7–9). 25:7–11 in a traditional number-saying emphasises the predominant importance of virtue as the basis for all human harmony. The reference to serving an inferior presumably refers to the pagan overlords.

Sir 25:13–26:4. Contrast the good and evil wife. There is nothing worse than the latter; it is like living with an implacable mortal enemy. Sirach describes how she drives out all joy from life, and eventually also her husband. In a final bitter remark (25:24), he blames woman for bringing death (Gen 3:12 f); if a wife will not take correction she should be divorced. Sirach definitely writes from the viewpoint of the dominant male, who would be disinclined to accept any responsibility for the unhappy situation; even the loyal wife is seen as essentially supportive, a blessing for her husband.

In 26:5–18, the numerical proverb focuses on the unreasonably jealous wife. This leads Sirach to consider the side-effects of this situation, the wife or daughter who attempts to redress the balance by becoming flirtatious, fighting masculine control by her promiscuity. For Sirach woman's place is very definitely in the home, where she should obey husband or father.

Sir 26:19–27:15. The proverb introduces a discussion of the occasions of sin. Success in business posed a particular temptation for Jews in the unsettled religious climate in Palestine, as it was all too likely they would have to adopt the methods of their irreligious competitors and desert the law for gain. The genuine man is known by his speech, this is the infallible test. If he seeks truth he will find it, as the honest man can never be exploited while the dishonest only finds dishonesty. The conversation of good men is edifying; that of fools purposeless.

Sir 27:16–28:26. Further counsels against disruptive and unproductive behaviour with friends and associates. Occasional abuse may be reconciled, but betrayal of confidences destroys the essential foundation of trust (cf 22:22 f). Still more is this true of the hypocrite; in accord with the law of inevitable retribution (27:25–27) deceit and dishonesty leads only to isolation. The wise man will not seek vengeance when wronged (cf Mt 6:12, 18:23–25), but will be faithful to mercy, as is the Lord. The quarrelsome man who concentrates on his own grievance will only find further frustration. Sirach concludes his analysis of man's divisive tendencies with another polemic on the tongue's potential for evil (cf Jas 3:1–12). Small communities are most vulnerable to slander, hence Sirach warns emphatically against loose talk.

Sir 29:1–28. The law commanded the Jews to lend money to fellow-Israelites if they needed it (Lev 25:35; Deut 15:7–11); but forbade them to exact any interest (Ez 22:25; Lev 25:36). Sirach reminds his well-to-do hearers of this injunction, also of their obligation to repay debts promptly, even if they are rich. He attempts, not altogether successfully, to counter the common argument that such loans are often wasted (29:4–7), then turns his

attention from loans to almsgiving. The truly generous
man will not expect any return on his loan but will seek
a different treasure (29:8–13, cf Mt 6:19 f; Lk 16:9).
While the earlier sages advised against accepting obliga-
tions on behalf of another (cf Prov 6:1 ff, 11:15, 17:18,
22:26), Sirach knows this can be a sign of generosity,
even though the pitfalls are many. It has ruined good
men as well as those who have sought to profit from it,
and so must be done cautiously. The poor man in turn
should preserve his independence, as the parasite loses
all dignity; he is at the mercy of the rich man or the
moneylender (29:21–28).

Sir 30:1–13. Sirach's attitude towards rearing children
is anything but permissive—this only leads to further unrest (30:7). Strong discipline enables a father to be proud
of his son, and ensures that the son will eventually be
grateful to his memory. Even if this does meet stubborn
resistance, the test of wills must always be resolved in the
parent's favour.

Sir 30:14–25. Physical and mental health are far better
than material goods. Without health wealth is useless, as
futile as trying to feed the dead or lifeless idols. The wise
man seeks contentment first of all (cf Eccl 2:24).

Sir 31:1–11. This leads Sirach to consider the futility of
the anxious and obsessive quest for money; it destroys
peace of mind and ruins a man's health. Indeed, love of
money causes spiritual ruin; the rich man who remains
blameless is so rare as to cause wonderment.

Sir 31:12–32:13. Sirach concludes this section with a
code of etiquette, concentrating on good manners at
table, especially in formal situations. He stresses moderation and restraint for the guest, and liberality for the

host; greed and meanness are both signs of selfishness. This is especially true with wine; taken in moderation it is excellent cheer, but only the fool thinks that the ability to drink much proves a man's worth. One who presides at table should not try to dominate but consider the good of all; the elderly must beware of becoming boring, the young of being arrogant. One should not linger too long in someone else's house, but return home where one can properly relax. Food and drink are basically good, and should lead to praise of God; this is the guiding principle, underlying the more practical advice.

1. *How acceptable is Sirach's concept of the marriage relationship?*

2. *'Sin is wedged in between selling and buying' (27:2)—is this general truth or mere disparagement of trade?*

Sir 32:14–33:18. The traditional introductory admonition, which introduces a fourth section, stresses discipline and fear of the Lord, the criteria for honest commitment. Sirach continues his polemic against the encroachments of hellenism; the true Israelite is deliberate in all his actions, relying on the law, infallible as a direct oracle, to guide and guard him, in contrast to the hypocritical apostate. In Israel's unsettled situation a certain amount of circumspection was all the more necessary, as ungodly men were in positions of power. Sirach accepts this fact as part of God's plan; as he made the days different, some of them solemn feasts and others mere units of time, so he has made men different even though all have the same origin. He outlines different groups in 32:12; respectively the Israelites, the levites and priests, and the despoiled Canaanites. All were subject to God's power; Sirach implies it will be the same for their successors in the present.

While men are different, the only absolute opposition is between good and evil; creation's contrasting categories are also signs of the completeness of God's plan (42:24). He concludes with a personal note; God has exalted him and given him some influence, but he uses this to invite others to wisdom, not seeking to preserve it for himself by reticence or accommodation to the foreign rulers.

Sir 33:19–31. Sirach resumes his particular counsels, stressing the proper use of authority. The influential man should always preserve his independence, and mastery over his family and household, till the very end. Slavery was taken for granted in Sirach's day, and he counsels exacting supervision; but he also recognises that a servant has a mind and dignity of his own, a remarkably enlightened attitude for the time.

Sir 34:1–17. Sirach contrasts the relative value of dreams and experience in understanding life. Dreams may occasionally bring insight, but cannot be relied on, as they often merely reflect one's own desires, and too easily result in self-deception. The strong man can face reality, and Sirach appeals to his wide experience of foreign customs and mores; while these have led him into danger, they have also brought much insight. He concludes with a hymn praising confidence in God, which ultimately saves the wise.

Sir 34:18–35:20. Dreams and experience are ways of different relative value whereby God communicates with man; man in turn tries to contact God through prayer and sacrifice. In the confused religious situation in Palestine, sincere devotion was all the more necessary to preserve true religion. Sirach attacks purely external practices; sacrifices without sincerity are unacceptable to

God, as there can be no compromise in worship. Sirach does not go as far as the prophets; he considers external worship necessary, and pleasing to God, as long as it accompanies righteous living. God cannot be bribed; he answers the prayer of the oppressed rather than the sacrifices of the rich. 35:18–20 shifts the thought to oppressed Israel, introducing a note of messianic hope; the Lord will eventually free Israel from her present affliction, because of the prayer of the pious.

Sir 36:1–17. Sirach then offers such a prayer, calling on God to destroy Israel's enemies (36:1–2, 6–10), show his mercy to Israel (36:1, 4, 11–14), and bring all men to recognise his lordship (36:4, 15–17). He prays that this will happen soon, in a rare reference to the messianic era (36:8), asking that the 'in-gathering' of the tribes from the diaspora, always regarded as a vestige of the punishment of exile, may manifest God's power and complete through Israel the promise made to all mankind (36:11, 15).

Sir 36:18–37:15. Sirach offers advice on choosing friends and associates—the basic principle, the need for discrimination, is stated in 36:18–20, followed by three examples, on choosing a wife, friends and advisers. According to oriental custom a woman had to accept the husband chosen for her; Sirach reminds his pupils of this advantage, warning them not to be hasty, but also not to delay too long. As for friends, he repeats his previous advice (6:5–17), and counsels against the self-seeking adviser, giving some practical examples. The virtuous man is most likely to be genuinely disinterested.

Sir 37:16–26. Sirach offers some principles for self-discernment, the basis of the self-reliance mentioned in 37:

13–14. Good and evil, life and death, have their origin in the heart, the seat of reason and intention, and are manifested through speech; the chiastic structure establishes the principle (37:17–18). He gives three examples of imperfect wisdom; the man who can counsel others but not himself, or who cannot communicate his knowledge and so cannot earn a living, or who needs no critic but himself. The true sage is able to make his wisdom productive; after death he earns a lasting memory, and while living shares in the permanence of Israel's tradition.

Sir 37:27–38:23. Sirach advises against over-indulgence in order to preserve one's health and ensure a long life, man's highest good. Some of the more pious considered consulting a doctor betrayed lack of confidence in God (2 Chron 16:21); Sirach emphasises that the doctor's skill is God's gift. Both the sick man and the physician pray for assistance, but the prayer should come first; the evil man will have only the doctor to help him when he falls sick. The same pragmatic advice covers mourning the dead (38:16–23); the ritual prescriptions should be observed (Ez 24:15–24), but not prolonged, as this diminishes and depresses the living unduly. Every man's time will come; there is no sense in dwelling on death.

Sir 38:24–39:11. Sirach's defence of the doctors leads him to compare the relative merits of the scholar and the artisan, as many of his contemporaries, not to mention many since, tended to disparage the tradesman, in order to enhance their own importance. Sirach is aware that society honours the learned and influential more than the workman, but insists that this is largely because they have the leisure time necessary to acquire wisdom. Originally, 'wisdom' meant skill or dexterity in any human activity, and in 38:31 Sirach's grandson uses the

Greek word for wisdom to refer also to the craftsman's skill. The craftsman structures society's foundations; he may not have time to philosophise but his careful work is itself a prayer of praise. The wise man provides an added cultural function, expanding man's spirit through his study of the scriptures (39:1) and other classics, his experience in affairs of state, and his prayer. This activity culminates in his own teaching and writing, in disseminating his insights for others' benefit. This may bring him fame; but the scribe's own reputation and honour is less important than the real benefits he provides for his fellows.

Sir 39:12–35. Sirach gives an example of the wise man's insight, focusing on the perennial problem of God's responsibility for good and evil. His basic presupposition is that of Genesis; everything God has created is good. He attacks undue speculation as to the purposes of God, of the type found in Qoheleth (39:17, cf Eccl 3:11); all will be revealed in due time. God does have a plan, to reward the just and punish the wicked; what seems evil to the wicked is in fact good; it is their due punishment, and is seen as such by holy men. Everything God does is good; Sirach concludes his confident assertion with a renewed exhortation to praise God for his creation.

Sir 40:1–41:13. Sirach is not unaware of suffering and pain; he counterbalances the optimism of his previous assertions with a meditation on the troubles of man, especially the existential evil of death (40:1–11). But while he recounts man's all-embracing problems (the seven evils in verse 4 indicate their completeness) which plague even the time of rest in sleep, he does not abandon the principle; all this is a result of sin, especially the sin of Adam. He alludes to Gen 3:17 in 40:1, 11; because of

the curse man must die and return to the earth, the
Hebrew word for which is *adam* (cf Gen 3:19–20)—the
Hebrew for 40:11 has 'what is from above returns above',
an allusion to the life-breath given by God. All men suffer
some of the consequences of this sin, but those who choose
sin deliberately find no escape from them, only inevitable
destruction (40:8–10). 40:12–17 combine traditional
maxims on the theme of retribution, followed by a series
of comparison-sayings (40:18–27) stressing personal
values and wisdom, culminating in fear of the Lord, the
basis of a true covenant-relationship with God. 40:28–30
reminds the pupils that begging brings resentment and
loss of self-respect.

Sirach offers further thoughts on death (41:1–4); the
man in the prime of life wants to hear none of it, while
the very old welcome it—the wise man at least must not
fear it, but accept it as a fact. Sinners will be cursed by
their children and die unremembered (41:5–13), subject
to the full weight of death's power. Sirach attacks those
who have renounced judaism for hellenism, forsaking all
claim to the promise (41:8).

Sir 41:14–42:14. Using his customary style of contrasting opposites (33:15, 42:24) Sirach compares true and
false shame (cf 4:20–28). Human respect played a large
part in facilitating the spread of hellenism especially
among the urban upper classes who were most susceptible to such influence. The first part (41:14–23) gives
seven examples of genuine shame, always relative to some
other person, culminating with the most important, respect for the law, behind which stands God. He mentions
some common violations and concludes with a reminder
that this is the way to find true honour. He then warns
against false shame, especially shame of one's religion (1

Mac 1:11–15). Building upon this theme, Sirach describes a father's worry for his daughter. While he perhaps overemphasises the shame brought upon the parents if a wilful daughter should become pregnant, an attitude that may partly cause headstrong behaviour, he does stress the danger of neglect, an even more common pitfall. The man who spends too much time in feminine company also invites comment in a society where the roles were strictly differentiated.

1. Does Sirach tend to overemphasise prudence and caution at the expense of genuine charity?

2. Does Sirach go too far in ruling out all questioning as to the goodness of creation? Is there a sense in which war and famine are never good?

In a final section (42:15 ff), Sirach turns from practical counsel to a lengthy hymn in praise of Israel's heroes. His purpose is to remind his hearers of God's continued care, shown in nature and history, implicitly elaborating on the theme of ch 24, that true wisdom belongs to Israel. This technique of historical review as a hortatory device is quite common in the later writings, especially Wis 10–19, Jdt 8:26–27, 1 Mac 2:51–64, Heb 11, Ac 7.

Sir 42:15–43:33. The hymn in praise of God's work in creation serves as the standard introduction in typical wisdom style. He opens by praising God's power and knowledge in general terms; God has established creation's order, knows it throughout, but has not revealed it even to the angels (42:17). The notion of God's creative word appears here for the first time (42:15), an idea developed in later Johannine theology; in the earlier writings wisdom is usually God's agent. The 'signs of the age' (42:18–19) are the heavenly bodies; they determine time, reveal the future, and manifest the coming of the messiah. 42:24 refers to the theory of opposites, reflected in some of Sirach's literary techniques, which manifested the completeness of creation (Eccl 3:1–8). He details nature's interaction, concluding with a summons to extravagant praise; God had revealed a little of this mystery to the wise, but this only serves to make them realise how much more they do not know.

Sir 44:1–15. Sirach introduces his apologetic eulogy of Israel's ancestors, who have received the gift of wisdom, demonstrated in their fidelity to the covenant, here not specified but including all the continuing promise of God to his people. He selects men and incidents to stress this theme, as a counterbalance to the wavering faith of his contemporaries. The 'famous men' are men of *ḥesed*, or covenant fidelity, who have kept their promise to God; it was at this time that the sect of the *hasidim*, or scrupulously devout, began to take shape (1 Mac 2:42, 7:13). He outlines various classes of men, leaders, artists, advisers and aristocrats, who attained a certain eminence and renown (44:2–6), but also stresses that many unheralded men have continued the covenant through their quiet devotion; they live on in their descendants to the present time. Thus all the pious partake in Israel's promise of glory.

Sir 44:16–23. The reference to Enoch does not fit naturally here, as this initial section concentrates on the early patriarchs with whom the first covenants were made. Noah preserved mankind because of his piety, and received the covenant of continuation (Gen 8:22, 9:6 ff); he was a type of the remnant through which the promise perseveres (Is 4:3 ff, 6:13; 1 Pet 3:20, 2 Pet 2:5). Abra-

ham kept God's laws, made an initial agreement, passed
the first test (cf 2:1 ff), and because of this was granted
the promise of land and offspring (Gen 15:1–16; 22:1–
19). Sirach combines the accounts of Genesis to illustrate
the covenant-process of initial agreement, trial, and
eventual fulfilment. The promise made to Abraham continued in Isaac and Jacob.

Sir 45:1–26. Sirach makes no mention of Joseph, who
usually figures prominently in these wisdom passages (cf
49:15); he concentrates instead on Moses, who received
the commandments of the Sinai covenant directly from
God, a sign of Israel's pre-eminence, and Aaron, the
founder of the cult. The lengthy description of Aaron's
vestments may simply reflect Sirach's reverence for the
cult, but his insistence on the value of liturgical worship
and the perpetuity of the levitical priesthood were
especially important at a time when the high priesthood
had become a political pawn (45:13, cf 2 Mac 4:13–17,
23–29); the mention of Phinehas, Aaron's successor, emphasises the true succession of the priestly covenant
through Aaron's descendants. The priests were also
responsible for teaching the people (45:17), especially in
times of difficulty (45:22). The mention of the Davidic
covenant supports the notion of blood-succession of Israel's rulers; the high priest was the leader of the Jewish
community at the time, and the office was already being
fought over (2 Mac 3). 45:26 is an exhortation addressed
to the high priest in Sirach's time.

Sir 46:1–20. Joshua won many battles because of his
fidelity, and so earned continuance of the promise for
Israel; a reminder to Sirach's contemporaries that God's
power triumphed over the pagan nations through his
faithful servants, a lesson that was to be borne out by the

Maccabees. Caleb and Joshua passed the test of fidelity when they returned from spying out the promised land (Num: 14:6–24); they were the only ones allowed to enter, a reminder to Jews contemplating the apparently all-pervasive power of the hellenistic rulers. The judges and Samuel were likewise faithful and finally victorious.

Sir 47: 1–25. Nathan prophesied David's line would always continue (2 Sam 7:8–16); David was a mighty warrior who embellished the liturgy, and when he sinned he repented (2 Sam 12:12–25). Solomon flourished as long as he listened to wisdom and piety; his life proved the validity of wisdom's teaching, as sensuality led him to sin, tarnished his memory, and brought disruption through his sinful progeny.

Sir 48: 1–16. Elijah stands in contrast to Israel's unfaithful kings, bringing down rightful punishment on them, destroying Israel's enemies through fire (1 Kg 17:1–18:40). Sirach refers to the current speculation that Elijah's return would herald the messianic era (cf Mt 17:10). 48:11 is uncertain, it may refer to Elisha, who alone saw Elijah transported to heaven (2 Kg 2:10–12), or else those who will see Elijah after his return. Elisha also stood fast against wicked rulers, and raised a dead man after his own death (cf 2 Kg 13:20–21).

Sir 48: 17–49: 10. After the northern exile (48:15–16), only two of Judah's kings are worthy of praise. Hezekiah fortified Jerusalem and withstood Sennacherib, at the behest of the faithful prophet Isaiah (2 Kg 18:13–19:27; Is 36–37), a further lesson for Sirach's contemporaries. 48:24–25 indicate that the book of Isaiah was already in its present form by this time. Josiah converted the people after the iniquities of Manasseh's reign (2 Kg 22–23), restoring reverence for the law. All the other kings of Judah sinned, and because of this the southern kingdom was given into exile, as Jeremiah predicted. Jeremiah himself suffered the fate of all righteous prophets (Wis 2:10 ff; 2 Mac 6–7; Mt 5:11 ff, 23:24; Lk 11:49).

Sir 49:11–13. Zerubbabel, Jeshua and Nehemiah restored the temple after the exile, and defended Israel's traditions against enemies without and the fainthearted within (Ezr 3:2; Hag 1:12; Zech 3:1; Neh 1:1, 3:1).

Sir 49:14–16. It is not clear why Sirach adds this brief note on the prehistoric patriarchs; he may have wished to end the series with Adam, and mention major figures, Enoch and Joseph, here paralleled in their death, who were the subject of popular legend. Enoch's mysterious death (Gen 5:24) made him, like Elijah, a prefigurement of the resurrection and forerunner of the messiah; Joseph was the type of the pious wise man (1 Mac 2:53; Ac 7:10).

Sir 50:1–24. Simon II, who reigned as high priest from 220–195, by his public works, leadership and dedication to the worship of God enables Sirach to bring the list of Israel's heroes into the memory of his contemporaries. The ritual describes the day of atonement, a post-exilic feast celebrating the removal of Israel's sins. This was the only day on which the high priest pronounced the holy name of Yahweh in blessing on the people (50:18–21). Simon's devotion and majesty epitomises the superiority of Israelite worship to Greek sacrifices, and also serves as an example to his successors.

Sir 50:22–29. Sirach concludes his praise with a prayer that past glories may revive in Israel; the numerical invective castigates the Edomites in Hebron, the Philistine cities which were centres of hellenistic influence, and the

Samaritans, whose temple and sacred books attempted to rival those of Israel (Jn 4). Sirach signs his work, repeating his fundamental, integrating purpose, to expound the fear of the Lord.

Sir 51:1–30. The book concludes with two appended poems, the first a psalm of thanksgiving for deliverance from danger (51:1–12), and the second an alphabetical poem on the way to acquire wisdom (51:13–30). It is not certain whether either or both were written by Sirach; the first psalm may refer to his deliverance from attacks by opponents of the schools, and the second describe his intense pursuit of wisdom, ending with an invitation to join the wisdom school and gain genuine riches and the promise of God. The term used in the Hebrew, *beth midrash*, later meant a school of instruction in the law; it is not certain whether Sirach refers to a distinct wisdom school at this time.

1. How does the history of the church illustrate the principle that fidelity to authentic tradition brings salvation?

2. What criteria would we look for today to determine genuine allegiance in similar situations?

The Wisdom of Solomon
Introduction

The Wisdom of Solomon, despite its name, is the last of the old testament books. It was written in Greek, in Alexandria, in the early first century BC. At that time, Alexandria flourished as the intellectual, commercial and cultural centre of the East. Inevitably, the large Jewish community in the city was heavily influenced by this fluid, fast-moving environment with its exciting developments in science and philosophy. Their prized cultural and religious identity was in danger of being swamped, as their language had already been. Heavily involved in commerce, they could not escape the attractions of the surrounding culture. The Jews in Palestine had already resisted strenuously, at considerable cost, the deliberate pattern of Hellenistic cultural assimilation set in motion by Alexander the Great and carried to extremes by Antiochus Epiphanes in the second century (cf 1 Mac 1:41–63). Mystery cults and polytheistic practices threatened their worship of the one God, pagan hedonism their ethical beliefs, and popular philosophies their unique world-view. Reason and faith were in conflict, and the Jews in the Alexandrian ghetto had already suffered much because of their refusal to be easily assimilated.

In this milieu, the struggle for radical and religious

identity resulted in some Jews abandoning their faith, while others called for a total separation from the pagan world. The author of the Book of Wisdom attempted a middle course in this first attempt at reconciling Greek philosophy and Hebrew faith, giving wisdom's traditional internationalism a new direction. The book is an apologia for judaism, using terminology familiar to educated Greeks, but emphasising the superiority of Israel's faith. The argument is double-edged, directed at Jew and Greek, reassuring the former and attempting to convince the latter. Since the trauma of exile, Israel's thinkers had moved away from their narrow nationalism to a consciousness of mission, of Israel's task to bring knowledge of the true God to the whole world—Wisdom marks the highpoint of this development (18:4).

Theologically, the book also represents a considerable advance on previous categories. The problem of retribution, of the due and recognisable reward of just and unjust, had long been a major preoccupation of the schools. Now it enters a new dimension, as the unequivocal acceptance of belief in life after death gave the traditional principle of vindication a new and absolute validity. While the apparent anomaly of the impious man's success in life still disturbed the schoolmen, it no longer presented quite the same inexplicable danger to faith. God's wisdom, already given personal qualities in Prov 1:8–9, Job 28, Bar 3:8–4:4, Sir 24, is identified with the Spirit of the Lord; active and available as God's gift, she is the dynamic link between God and man, the agent of his creation. Wisdom lies behind Greek science (7:17–20) and cosmology (7:23–24), and is the source of the cardinal virtues of the stoics (8:7). There is thus no reason for the Jews to feel their wisdom is in any way inferior to that of the pagans. Israel's history, particularly at the exodus, demonstrates the superiority and permanence of God's power; as the Jews were once delivered from subjugation to Egyptian rule, they need not be afraid in the present. Loosely combining and expanding various biblical texts in midrashic style, the author relates Israel's past glory to the present situation of the Jewish community, in a savage polemic against idolatry. God's saving power contrasts with the impotence of idols.

The book consists of three sections, quite clearly distinguished from each other. 1:1–6:21 is written in homiletic style, and is concerned principally with reinforcing wavering faith. The author attacks apostate Jews and the community's persecutors, castigating all who seek short-term benefits and have abandoned their covenant promises. While the controversy regarding life after death was by no means settled in Israel, the author grounds his theodicy on this belief, especially against those who have distorted arguments similar to those used by Qoheleth (2:1–9). Barrenness (4:1–6) and early death (4:7–19), major tragedies for traditional faith, become credible or at least acceptable, as life is completely equated with virtue. In the second section (6:22–9:18), the author uses the legend of Solomon's wisdom to describe wisdom's nature and work in the world, emphasising her practical, concrete benefits and superiority to Greek wisdom, as the source of all real power and influence. In the final section (10:1–19:22), wisdom's action in salvation history demonstrates God's preserving power. God's wisdom, almost his cunning, appears in seven antitheses, where the means of salvation for the faithful Israelites at once punishes and destroys the idolatrous Egyptians. A long digression on the futility of idols (13–15) points up God's power reaching into their present situation, sustaining Israel's continuing hope.

Wisdom's somewhat hectoring style and unfamiliar philosophical terminology make it in some ways less appealing than the other wisdom books with their more obviously human concern. Its value lies mainly in its attempt to grapple with the problem of faith's role in structuring the experiences of life. The possibility and dimensions of ongoing life, the reality of suffering, the conflict of faith and reason, faith and cultural context remain current concerns. Wisdom's author shows faith and reason converging, becoming mutually supportive as he mellows extreme concern for religious tradition by his openness to valid human insight.

1. In what ways is modern man's faith a product of cultural presuppositions and behaviour-patterns rather than their determinant?

2. How can sacred history be usefully related to modern experience to support faith in the continued power of God?

3. What is the special nature of wisdom's power?

12

Wisdom and life
Wis 1:1–6:22

Wis 1:1–15. Introductory admonition

Wisdom's standard introductory warning to persevere in the search for justice here applies particularly to the rampant discontent and unrest in the Alexandrian ghetto. It is addressed to rulers, a common literary device in prophetic and wisdom exhortations—here the author has in mind the whole community, but especially its leaders, the elders and the wise, who were mainly responsible for maintaining covenant fidelity. Faith was most threatened by the querulous attitude first manifested by the people of God in Sinai, immediately after the exodus. The author reminds his audience that genuine fidelity must be tested; that any attempt to make demands on God will block any possibility of a fruitful relationship with him. Sincerity and integrity are absolute preconditions if the covenant promises are to be realised. Man's relationship with God is effected through wisdom, equated with the dynamic active spirit linking God and man, operating at the deepest level of personal being. The author uses the Greek idea of spirit as a kind of world-soul, binding the whole of creation together; it is also discipline, not in the Hebrew sense of restraint but the Greek notion of the condition for personal growth. Because of God's pervasive spirit deception

222

is futile, leading ultimately to death; while wisdom produces life, here given a pregnant sense; the totality of a life linked to God, fundamentally creative and undying, resulting in justice, the complete human harmony which is the end product of the covenant promise as well as man's search.

1. *Do we expect too much from God or can we hold him to his promises?*
2. *How is the Spirit the link between God and man?*

Wis 1:16–2:24. First speech of the wicked

These are apostate Jews who had rejected true wisdom with its broad understanding of life and opted for the world's more immediate rewards. Their efforts are shown to be short-sighted, as they negate life and produce only empty death. The author presents their practical atheism in the form of a speech (2:1–20); first setting out their limited view of life, then detailing the resulting acrimony and disharmony. Wis 2:1–9 is almost a caricature of some aspects of Qoheleth's thoughts, without any echo of his compensating faith; concentration on the enjoyment of one's work has become the unrelenting search for pleasure. The author is possibly refuting those who use his awareness of life's finite limits as an excuse for unbridled self-seeking. Wis 2:10–20, where the apostates resolve to vent their basic uncertainty on the poor just man, is reminiscent of the fourth servant song (Is 52:13–53:12). The author probably has in mind a typical pious teacher, who was not interested in the search for wealth but was totally concerned to maintain the traditions of Israel's faith and piety in the schools. His only power lay in his word and example, hence his rebukes were all the more objectionable to those who had deserted this faith. Indirectly it refers to the whole faithful community, which stood as a perpetual reproach to the apostates.

Final vindication for the pious faithful lies in the future; the references to Gen 1:26; 3 shows that the author has in mind more than the simple continuance of life. He does not say that immortality is natural to man; it is the result of God's promise and is earned by fidelity. Physical death results from man's earthly nature, spiritual death comes from sin. Hence physical death has no power over those who remain faithful to God; the wicked men's attempt to kill the just man shows that they have missed the point, the secret of true wisdom is hidden from them (cf 2 Mac 7:14, 26 ff).

1. How effectively can we argue for or against life after death?

2. Is human weakness always powerless? How is its power made constructive rather than destructive?

3. How much proof do we need of God's power?

Wis 3:1–4:19. The secrets of true wisdom

The author outlines fortune's reversal through faith. The just live with God—this is the secret of true wisdom, and it offers the solution to three classic problems—the just still may suffer, be deprived of the blessing of children or die young. These are presented in the form of antitheses; the statement of faith contrasted with the consequences of unbelief.

Wis 3:1–12. The suffering of the just

The just may suffer and die, and in traditional terms this

could only be regarded as a punishment for sin. In the light of the author's faith, their sufferings are incommensurate with the reward for their fidelity. Their hope is not hopeless, as men think, but is the way to peace. The long-standing theory that sufferings test the just and confirm their faith gains new meaning—they are also a purification making the just ready for life with God. (8:2–5; Prov 3:11–12; Sir 2:1–6, 4:17–19.) The final judgement becomes their moment of total vindication; they inherit the full range of God's covenant promise to Israel as a result of their tested trust.

For those who have repudiated this trust, have lost faith, all is lost. For them death is total punishment. They have refused to listen to the teachers, have scorned the discipline of the schools and the careful, painstaking quest for honesty and integrity. As a result, their life is barren, all their hopes are doomed to frustration (cf the contrasting effects of the servant's death in Is 53:10–12). Even their natural ambitions for their family result in total disappointment, as their influence is wholly negative.

 1. Should faith depend on the expectation of future reward?
 2. Can suffering usefully be regarded as a test sent by God?
 3. Must the just always suffer?

Wis 3:13–4:6. Childlessness

The author contrasts the brood of the wicked with the situation of the just who have no children. He follows the sequence in Is 54:1, 56:2–5, where descendants are promised to barren Jerusalem. In traditional Hebrew thought, children were a sign of God's blessing, of the permanence of his promise, while sterility indicated his curse. The value of a man's life was asserted ultimately through his children, who preserved his memory. The author attacks this primary attitude to demonstrate the radical nature of his conception of life. He does not sublimate the promise of children, but points to a different reward, a deeper fruitfulness in the continuance of God's promise in the lives of those faithful to him.

The adulterers are those who have renounced their faith; since they have deprived their children of meaningful faith and a share in the covenant promises, they incur the real curse, blighting their descendants' lives as well as their own.

4:1–6 reaffirms the principle; childlessness with virtue is better than children without it. The importance of children is maintained, but the whole, virtuous life has its unique value. It lives in men's memories, but more importantly shares in God's permanence. The children of the wicked lack this permanence and confidence—in any testing situation they have nothing to fall back on, their confusion makes their parents' lack of preparation manifest to all. In this way the parents' sin is visited on their offspring (cf Sir 41:5–7; Jn 9:2) and the parents' wickedness immortalised.

1. Can parents be said to be responsible for their children's values and mistakes?

2. What does the Hebrew conception of the role of children as a sign of the covenant add to modern debates about birth control and abortion?

3. What insight does this passage offer to those who lead a single life?

Wis 4:7–19. Early death

Traditional Hebrew morality promised long life as a reward for virtue. While this implied more than simply reaching a great age, early death, especially for the promising, capable youth remained an anomaly. The man who died young could not obtain the fulness of the covenant promises, in fact he seemed to be excluded from them, which should have been the fate of the wicked. The author again stresses the absolute importance of virtue as the criterion of genuine life, avoiding temporal categories completely. Growth to full maturity in virtue normally takes a lifetime; if it comes early, this is already a true 'old age'. The author uses the example of Enoch (Gen 5:24; Sir 44:16; Heb 11:5) as an illustration—by snatching him away God prevents any possibility of future sin by denying the promise. He attacks the basic lack of insight, the superficial attitude of those who do not see the supreme importance of virtue and are confused by death, seeing it as a sign of wisdom's ineffectualness. This lack of true insight makes their own death, at no matter what age, truly empty and ineffectual.

1. Can early death in any sense be considered a blessing?
2. Is immortality consoling?

Wis 4:20–5:23. The final judgement: second speech of the wicked

In the final judgement the tables are completely turned; the just man whom the wicked had considered powerless and foolish becomes their confident powerful prosecutor. The dramatic courtroom encounter sets the scene, but the author concentrates especially on the wicked men's 'anguish of spirit'. They see how foolish they have been, as the just man's life style is finally vindicated, and their own revealed to be totally null and purposeless. Life after death is described through the traditional imagery of the heavenly court. The 'sons of God' are both the just, who have built a special relationship with God by their fidelity to the covenant (cf 2 Sam 7:14), and the angels in the heavenly court (Job 1:6). The just share in the angelic intimacy with God.

5:15–23 returns to the theme of 1:13–14, describing the struggles of the just before the final judgement. They already live with God, and share in his power. As they become whole and integral themselves through their relationship with God, all of his creation works to benefit in total harmony. God himself fights for them (Is 59:16–17) and so they already possess life in its totality; whereas the wicked will be effectively annihilated at the end.

1. Is it ever possible to turn away from God with full deliberation?

2. Is the final judgement simply a manifestation of basic attitudes?

Wis. 6:1–21. Renewed exhortation to seek wisdom

The author rounds out this initial section by expounding on his opening theme (1:1–4); here however he addresses the gentile 'kings' rather than the Israelite 'judges'. They too must seek wisdom and virtue, for ultimately their power derives from the God Israel knows (Prov 8:15; Jn 19:11). They are not exempt from his judgement, in fact the author warns them of impending calamity because they have not kept God's laws. He uses the imagery of the traditional power-struggle between spiritual wisdom and earthly might (Prov 24:5; Eccl 9:13–15). God's power vindicates the poor and the weak in spite of overwhelming odds, through the wisdom, strength of purpose and shrewdness that come with virtue. Superficial strength leads to overweening arrogance, and is often thus made powerless, especially when resisted or tested. True power is interior, given by God as a result of virtue, and is backed up by the supreme power of God. Wisdom consequently does not need any external show of strength, but confidently makes herself available to all as the source of true power (cf Prov 1:20–21; 8:1–36). The final sorites (6:17–20) summarises the process leading from the desire for wisdom to true power—ultimately this is realised in the eschatological reign with God. The author transcends the limits of traditional wisdom, addressed particularly to kings and administrators, showing them the way to establish a stable kingdom; wisdom is available to all, and in effect makes all men rulers (3:8).

1. How can we assess the effects of wisdom's power?

2. Should we always vote for the man and not the party? How important is a leader's personal life as a sign of his capacity to rule?

3. Does every man need to be powerful?

13

The search for wisdom's nature
Wis 6:22–9:18

Wis 6:22-25. Introduction

The author takes on Solomon's persona in this section, underlining his political concern. Solomon was not only revered as a wise man, but also ruled an expanding Israel at the zenith of her power; the author assumes his transferred authority in describing the nature of true wisdom. Her origin is mysterious (7:25–26, cf Job 20:20–28), hidden in God. The mystery cults revealed their secrets only to initiates, this was one source of their power; the philosophers too did not wish their insights to be widely circulated and diluted. Wisdom on the contrary, while mysterious, needs no artificial support or jealous retention; she is truly self-sufficient, and must be disseminated as widely as possible. The prologues to Proverbs and Sirach, also Eccl 12:9, underline the expansionist ambitions of the later schools, in contrast to practical wisdom's emphasis on reticence (Prov 12:23).

Wis 7:1–8:21. The speech of Solomon

Wis 7:1-6. Mortal Solomon

Although wisdom ultimately derives from God, she is available to all men. Solomon emphasises the common circumstances of his birth and eventual death to underline the fact that he had no special prerogatives as king when he began his search. He does not claim divine origin or knowledge as did other oriental rulers.

Wis 7:7–22. Solomon prays for wisdom

Solomon chose wisdom ahead of wealth (1 Kg 3:4–9); as a reward he receives riches as well (1 Kg 3:10–14). His prayer is recounted in Wis 9. Here the author emphasises, for his own pedagogical purposes, that Solomon prayed for wisdom, whereas in the earlier account God simply offered him a reward for performing his duties, and Solomon chose wisely. This ideal picture is elaborated, Solomon shares this gift ungrudgingly. Wisdom leads to wealth; therefore wisdom must be sought first of all, even when the connexion is not apparent.

The literary fiction is carried further in 7:15–22; Solomon prays for help to speak convincingly about wisdom. This reflects the sage's own preoccupation; for although Solomon had extensive knowledge of nature (1 Kg 4:32–34), he is represented here as proficient in all the sciences, from astronomy to medicine, which flourished in hellenistic times. Natural cycles and powers fascinated the ancient world, shaping their view of religion and history, but the sage emphasises the supremacy of God's wisdom, creating and directing man and nature according to his purpose.

1. Is the search for wisdom all that is necessary?

2. How does God 'answer' prayer—should we pray for things to change or only that we may do so?

3. Is prayer dialogue or monologue?

Wis 7:22–8:1. The nature and dignity of wisdom

Wisdom's work in the world is described in terms borrowed from the Greek philosophers; the 21 attributes express her completeness, as a multiple of 7 (perfection) and 3 (the divine number). The Greeks conceived of *Nous* or *Logos* as a kind of world soul, material yet subtle and all-pervading. This total immanence also belongs to spiritual wisdom, linking the world to God. Two attributes receive special mention; wisdom's omnipresence, reflecting the total power and presence of God; and her spiritual power, inspiring and protecting holy men, prophets and leaders, who cannot be defeated by the powers of darkness. Wisdom is always totally creative.

Wis 8:2–21. Wisdom, the source of blessings

This chapter is constructed in the form of a chiasmic elaboration on 7:1–22. The author first describes the blessings wisdom brought Solomon (8:2–8), adapting the traditional figure of the beautiful young bride, perhaps to canonise his well-known romantic propensities (1 Kg 3:7; Ps 44:5–10). This image had already been used to describe the relation between Israel and Yahweh (cf Hos 1–3); it is continued now in his gift of wisdom. Wisdom leads to wealth and renown: as Solomon was internationally famous for his wisdom, so the Jews should not be ashamed of their wisdom compared with that of the contemporary philosophers and scientists. Wisdom stands behind the goals of good men of all nations, for she too teaches prudence and temperance, justice and fortitude, the cardinal virtues of Plato and the stoics (8:7).

Since wisdom is the source of all genuine knowledge, Solomon seeks her as his adviser and comforter (8:9–16). The author attacks overemphasis on intellectual pursuits; for wisdom brings a deeper insight, the capacity to judge rightly. This wins the lasting approval of men, the ancient concept of immortality (8:13), and is the source of true power. Wisdom is pictured in traditional terms, in the role of king's counsellor, taking always a long-range view, bringing consolation in time of setback, reminding the king of eventual triumph.

The key to obtaining wisdom is to recognise it as God's gift (8:17-21, cf 7:1-6); it does not come automatically, nor is it the result of natural gifts. The author attacks the philosophers' rationalism, claiming wisdom as their due. The Greek reverence for intellect and speculative enquiry brought many benefits to man, but true wisdom fits this into the larger pattern of faith and reverence for God. Wis 8:20 does not necessarily imply any theory of the human soul's pre-existence, the author simply wishes to correct any impression from the preceding verse that the soul is inferior to the body. The Greeks considered that the soul was encased in an impure body and strove to escape from this prison. The author does not accept this framework, as other places show (1:4-14, 2:23-24, 7:20, 15:11); he insists that Solomon, though particularly gifted, still had to pray for wisdom.

1. Does our culture value intelligence and education too highly at the expense of wisdom and experience?

2. Are we still influenced by the notion that the body is evil?

3. Is scientific progress always wise?

Wis 9:1-18. Solomon's prayer

This chapter is modelled on Solomon's famous prayer at the dedication of the first temple (1 Kg 3:6-9). Solomon asks for wisdom because he is a man (9:1-6), and because God has made him king (9:7-12). He addresses the

God of Israel, the God of his fathers who established a special relationship with the Jews through the covenant of mercy. He is also the creator-God, who intended man to rule the created world in harmony with the laws he established. Solomon knows his own weaknesses, the weakness of all men, and asks for wisdom to discern this harmony, to establish the pattern willed by God. Even the perfect man needs this extra dimension which comes directly from God. As king, Solomon must also support God's plan for his people, in work and worship. This too he can only do through God's wisdom; the harmony of creation and God's plan for Israel are facets of the one divine purpose for all mankind. He elaborates this into a general principle in the concluding section (9:13–18). All human knowledge is insecure—the author adapts the terminology of platonic dualism without accepting the implication that matter is evil, simply that the earth-bound body weighs down the soul (Job 4:19; Ps 103:14; 38:12; Rom 7:14–25). Man's limitations make it difficult to structure his own environment, only God can reveal the divine master-plan. All men thus need true wisdom; and she has already been revealed in Israel's history. Wis 9:18 marks the transition to the final section, calling the Alexandrians to witness this fact.

1. How is human weakness transformed by divine wisdom?

2. Does our spirituality emphasise perfection rather than self-acceptance?

3. How far does psychology threaten faith?

14
Wisdom in history
Wis 10:1–19:22

From the beginning of time wisdom protected and saved her followers. The author elaborates on this principle, stated at the beginning of the book (1:2–3:1). He uses scripture extensively, combining selected passages out of their historical context, embellishing them with popular legends and personal insights, in traditional midrashic style. No names are mentioned, to give the principle wider application; every example contrasts the fate of the just with that of the godless wicked. He concentrates on the exodus narrative, the principal manifestation of God's power in Egypt. He promises the complete vindication of Israel's faith in the coming judgement, for the Jewish religion is immeasurably superior to the empty idolatry current in Alexandria; Yahweh was and is powerful, active and concerned for his people.

Wis 10:1–21. Introduction

This chapter marks a transition from the call to wisdom and the general statement in 9:18, to detailed consideration of the exodus. The author compresses patriarchal history, focusing on Adam (10:1–2); Cain (10:3); Noah (10:4); Abraham (10:5); Lot and his wife (10:6–8); Jacob and Esau (10:10–12); Joseph (10:13–14) and Moses (10:16). He first describes individual men living

in a wicked world, ending with the general principle in
10:9; then the beginnings of the nation of Israel in
Egypt, leading to the deliverance of the 'holy and blameless people' (10:15). Current beliefs, of Adam's repentance (10:2); of the smoking, misty salt-flats and inedible
plants in the Dead Sea area that were considered to result from Sodom's destruction (10:7); of the plundering
of the drowned Egyptians by the Israelites (10:20) are
all combined with the biblical record. The author occasionally distorts the passage of history when he makes
Cain's sin the cause of the flood (10:4). Throughout,
wisdom guides and protects the just from their enemies,
giving them wealth and power; this is the foundation of
their continuing praise of God.

*1. Does modern history, or biography, reveal the wisdom of
God?*
2. Must the wicked always be punished?

Wis 11:2–19:22. God delivers Israel in Egypt

An extended meditation on God's fidelity to Israel, manifested once already in Egypt (11:5), sets the theme; the
very means God used to strengthen his people became a
punishment for their enemies. This section is possibly a
passover sermon; the author selects various details of the
exodus narrative to make his points. The people, familiar
with the general story, would readily appreciate the particular cast of his thought.

Wis 11:2–14. First antithesis, the power of water

Wis 11:2–4. Introduces the saga of the desert journey,
immediately reminding the listeners of the whole account. The people's primary need and first request was

for water; this God gave them from the rock, while the Egyptian's water source, the perennial Nile, the regular basis of their prosperity, turned to blood. According to the author, this resulted from the pharaoh's initial decree to kill the first-born Israelite males (Ex 1:16); in Ex 7:14 it is one of the plagues inducing pharaoh to let them leave Egypt. The author adapts the traditional thesis that God corrected and disciplined Israel through affliction, but destroyed her enemies—but he makes no mention of Israel's discontent. The Egyptians are said to have recognised the hand of God as well as the Jews; while there is no mention of this in the earlier tradition, it presumably is meant to strike home to the Alexandrians. To the Egyptians' discomfort in the land of plenty is added chagrin at seeing their enemies refreshed in the desert. The tables are turned completely; Moses, once rejected by Egypt, is vindicated in Israel.

Can sermons validly reflect a preacher's own predilections?

Wis 11:15–16:15. Second antithesis, the power of animals

This is presented in three sections: 11:15–16, 12:23–27, 15:18–16:4, all followed by digressions on true and false worship. The quails which fed the Israelites in the desert contrast with the small animals which plagued the Egyptians. This leads the author to compare God's power with that of the Egyptian idols, which often took animal form.

Wis 11:15–16. Statement of the theme

The Egyptians worshipped crocodiles and lizards, and used scarabs as magic charms. The plagues of locusts, frogs and mosquitoes are thus appropriate punishment for their mindless animal cults. In the old testament view, sin carried its own punishment with it (Ps 7:14–16; Prov 26:27; Mac 9:6).

Wis 11:17–12:22. God's power and mercy

The aptness of this method of reward and punishment leads the author into a discussion of God's way of acting with man and the world. God is all-powerful (11:17–20); he could have created savage and fierce monsters to punish his enemies, but in fact he has remained within his own limits, to demonstrate his mercy (11:23–12:2). He does not interfere unnecessarily in creation, being confident of power he has no need to show it off—the author defends the possibility of miraculous divine intervention against the Greeks, but looks to a deeper pattern in God's actions. He is perhaps reacting against the extremist apocalyptic language fashionable in certain circles, depicting savage cosmic conflicts and bitter destruction for the enemies of Israel or a particular sect. These too attempted to predict and thus set limits to God's power.

The author's eirenic, moderate concern tempers the impatience of those eager to see their opponents immediately thwarted. God is merciful (11:23–12:2); he acts gradually for he understands man's weakness and allows him time to repent. God is usually more merciful than man, as the gospels attest. This applies even to those outside Israel; here the author departs radically from the traditional theory of affliction as medicinal correction for Israel and punitive destruction for outsiders. God loves the whole of his creation; by implication man can hardly do any less. He created all men not only to live beyond death, but to live the full life of faith; hence he does not want to destroy any of his creation, for all possess his spirit. This universal understanding of the call to holiness takes old testament revelation to a new level and prepares for the gospel proclamation.

The universal providence of God is exemplified in Israel's history, in the treatment of the Canaanites (12:3–22). They occupied Palestine before Israel, were only gradually conquered, being in part assimilated into the new nation. Even though the pious might expect them to be exterminated immediately because of their inhuman practices, in fact their conquest was gradual and not without difficulty. The inference is that this is also God's method in Alexandria; the descriptions of Canaanite religious practices resemble initiation rites of the mystery cults, and the 'murderers of children' possibly refer to the Carthaginian Moloch-worship, practised to some extent in Alexandria. God does not condone these practices, but overcomes them gradually, providing time for them to repent, preferring conversion to destruction. God's leniency does not imply weakness, through lack of power or undue respect of persons (12:9–11). He is aware that ignorance excuses from guilt (12:15); secure in his power, in contrast to the wicked, he prefers to be lenient (12:16), establishing true justice (cf the contrast with the power of the wicked 2:11). Only those who wilfully disbelieve incur his full power—for they deny it fundamentally, a concept similar to the new testament sin against the Spirit (Mk 12:31; Lk 12:10). The author opposes self-satisfied separation; since God has acted mercifully towards the Israelites, they must be well-disposed to the gentiles.

Wis 12:23–27. Second statement of example

The Egyptians were punished by the very animals they idolised; they recognised the true God to some extent in Israel's vindication and the childish and superficial nature of their own beliefs, but in spite of this did not repent, hence they would experience the final condemnation.

    1. Are miracles signs of immature faith?

    2. Has christian theology and practice undervalued the mercy of God?

    3. What would Wisdom's author make of the argument that a good God should not allow evil?

Wis 13:1–15:17. Digression on false worship

The author tries to bring the Egyptians to a full recognition of the folly of idolatry, at the same time warning the Jews against it.

Wis 13:1–9. Attack on nature worship

The author does not attempt to prove the existence of God from nature, as all men accepted the reality of a supreme being or beings. The question is rather one of identification, of going beyond the wonders of nature to their maker. For the Jews, God revealed his power and purpose in Israel's history, manifesting his name and nature to Moses on Mt Sinai (Ex 3:14). The Greeks sought God through philosophical enquiry, and the author here accepts this as a valid approach to the God of Israel also (cf Rom 1:19–25). He seems to identify Yahweh, the 'He who is' of Israel, with the eternal being and source of beauty of platonic speculation, transcending the scope of Exodus. He is sympathetic towards their goal as well as their methods, and aware of the grandeur of nature that led them to stop short of the final comprehensive step; but he borrows their own concept of 'analogy' to emphasise that they must go further, to see that creation implies complete being.

Wis 13:10–15:17. The emptiness of idols

The philosophers are less blameworthy than those who fashion their gods themselves, for they are two dimensions removed from reality. Their judgement is more severe, their search and hope utterly futile. His scornful satire recalls the attacks of Is 44:9–20 and Bar 6, also some of the Greek philosophers. Even if the idols only represent the gods, these are as powerless as the wood because they are man-made projections. The artisan's skill, an age-old synonym for wisdom, may cover the idol's blemishes, but is completely powerless to save him, in contrast to true wisdom. The father's providence, another term borrowed from the philosophers (14:1 ff), is the seafarer's only salvation, an allusion to Noah and the exodus. God's real power is revealed in Israel's history; the frail wood of the ark preserved Noah, and so mankind (14:6); but wooden idols have only led men to destruction, hence idols and their makers are both accursed. The christian fathers applied this text to the wood of the cross.

Wis 14:12–31. The origins and consequences of idolatry

Idols are basically false, a denial of life. Those who make them cannot be honest, they have to pretend that the time-limited is eternal. The author gives two examples of how idols originate; a king makes an image of his dead son, and orders its veneration; or a clever artist fashions a statue of a king who lives in a distant city. Emperor-worship was rife throughout the East, especially in Egypt; the artist's ambition feeds this unnatural cult, his skill is seen as a sign of the idol's divinity. The author points up the consequences of the basic falsity; while it may be inspired by the need to structure harsh realities of life, it only leads to greater corruption. The Jews, accustomed to a strict moral code, must have been appalled by the moral laxity often fostered by the various cults. Since even their devotees did not expect real help from their gods, they compounded the basic falsity of their devotion by swearing false oaths, destroying all possibility of order and cooperation in society. Defenceless against themselves, idol-worshippers have no defence against each other; they can only escape by frenzied search for pleasure or cold exploitation.

Wis 15:1–6. The true worship of Israel

Israel's God is real; his people know him as a person, understanding and patient. If they should sin, they know he will be merciful, but because they know and trust him, they do not want to break off their personal relationship with him by sin. This personal relationship with the living God is the basis for all ethics, as it is in the new testament; it leads to genuine life through the saving power of God, made manifest in Israel's history.

Wis 15:7–17. The potter and his clay

The potter's crime is even worse than the carpenter's, for he alone determines the purpose of his pottery. His craft contrasts with God's creative power, where he breathed life into lifeless clay (Gen 2:7 f). The potter, himself fashioned from the earth, has no power to enliven his product; in deceiving himself he denies his own life, perverting its purpose by not only not considering this but unashamedly working for money—he even gilds the clay to compete with the goldsmiths. In trying to 'make a living' he denies himself all prospect of a genuine life (15:12). The Egyptians accepted and venerated all these idols, even the gods of other nations, an inconceivable practice for the Jews with their understanding of the personal bond between Israel and Yahweh.

Wis 15:18–16:15. Third statement of example

The mention of the Egyptians, 'the enemies of the people', (15:14), leads the author back to the question of their animal-worship and its consequences. The pests afflicting Egypt contrast with the quail provided for Israel in the desert (Ex 16:9–13). Egypt, the land of plenty, was struck by famine, as the animals plaguing them were as repellent as their bizarre deities. Even when the Jews themselves are bitten in the plague of serpents, it was only for a short while, and they were given a sign of salvation, the serpent Moses mounted on a staff (Num 21:4–9). The author is extremely careful to point out that God and not the serpent saved the Israelites. The people's short affliction stimulates their faith, giving evidence of deliverance, whereas the Egyptians' vaunted skill in medicine could not save them from death. God's word and power alone has ultimate dominion over man's life, for he can render snake venom harmless; on the contrary, man can kill but cannot bring anyone back to life.

1. Does the idea of creation have any value for apologetic today?

2. Do we still fashion idols? Have they any sense of transcendence?

3. Why is it a wisdom all sublime, to make the punishment fit the crime?

Wis 16:16–29. Third antithesis, the reversal of the elements

The scribal love of elaborate symbolism is obvious in this passage. The Egyptians are not only afflicted by rain and hail, but also by lightning which passes through the rain unquenched, setting fire to their food crops but leaving untouched the plaguing animals. The natural prevalence of fire in thunderstorms becomes a sign of God's providence, a reminder to the Jews in Alexandria that the whole of nature is on their side (5:20, 10:20). In contrast, the manna which fed the Israelites in the desert looked like frost (16:22) yet did not melt when cooked. Fire in the old testament is a common sign of destruction and punishment; but for the Israelites, God removed this quality as a reminder that nature worked for the just, and also that God's word rather than ordinary food provides man's true nourishment (Deut 8:3; Mt 4:4). However the manna did melt in the sun; the Jews should therefore express their dependence on God's word by their morning and night prayer before sunrise and after sunset, as this alone can sustain their hope.

1. How narrow is the line between superstition and faith?
2. Can the poor live by the word of God?

Wis 17:1–18:4. Fourth antithesis, light and darkness

The ninth plague, of darkness over the land of Egypt (Ex 10:23 ff), immobilised the people in a prison without bars and so was fitting punishment for their refusal to release the Israelites. For the Jews in Alexandria, the author extends the symbol—mental darkness and blind terror punish the pagans' secret sins, committed in darkness, probably a reference to bizarre initiation rites in the mystery cults (1:7–10:8). What light there was in Egypt (the intermittent fires indicate lighting) only enhanced the darkness; their magicians were proved powerless, some even dying of fright. He also broadens the general principle of the punishment inherent in sin, introducing the notion of conscience for the first time in the bible. Sin shows its true self in confusion and distortion when trouble comes, creating problems where none exist because of a guilty conscience. This leads him to a short disquisition on fear, the complete surrender to the irrational (17:12–15) which feeds upon uncertainty, succumbing to what is essentially powerless. Only the Egyptians experienced this darkness, yet it was the interior emptiness which troubled them most, making ordinary sounds full of horror.

In contrast, the Israelites had light in the land of Egypt (Ex 10:23), and the pillar of fire to lead them through the desert. The Egyptians heard the Israelites but could not see them; thanked them for not taking advantage of their plight and pleaded with them to intercede with God. This interaction is not in the original account, it rather reflects the author's apologetic purpose. Egypt was justly punished by the lack of light, but this was only to prepare them for the light of the law, which they hopefully will yet receive. Wis 18:4 is the clearest statement of the universal potential of Israel's faith in the old testament. The law is called light in previous wisdom books (Prov 6:23; Sir 45:21); here it is meant for all men and not only for favoured Israel (Is 42:6, 51:4).

1. *Is all fear irrational?*
2. *What is the relation between neurosis and faith?*

Wis 18:5–19:22. Fifth antithesis: the fate of the first-born

This section returns to the basic questions of true life and death running throughout the book. Two major antitheses are presented: the plague of the first-born sons is a punishment for the pharaoh's decree to kill the first-born male Israelites; and the rescuing of Moses and others from drowning in the Nile contrasts with the destruction of the Egyptian army in the Red Sea. 18:5 introduces the antithesis, cutting across the comparisons by linking the Red Sea disaster to the pharaoh's decree and Moses' rescue.

Wis 18:6–25. The death of the first-born

18:6–9 describes the people celebrating the passover ritual, secure in the promise of God's protection. God promised the patriarchs he would deliver their descendants (Gen 15:13–14; 46:3–4); the author says he revealed this incident to them to strengthen their covenant-faith. By implication, the original passover should encourage the Alexandrian Jews who also faced opposition in Egypt. They praise the faith of the patriarchs (instead of the usual *Hallel*, Pss 113–118), and await release. In contrast the Egyptians wail and lament as their children die (18:10–19). Although the magicians could reproduce the earlier plagues, they were powerless against death (17:7–10), and were forced to recognise the Israelites as God's sons (Ex 12:31), the term applied to the just man in 2:16 (cf Ex 4:22 f, 12:31). God's powerful word carried out his judgements; the passage is applied to the incarnation in the Roman liturgy. As the Egyptian children lay dying, they too recognised the presence of God in their final fearful visions (cf Job 4:13–15).

18:20–25 meets possible objections that God also punished Israel with death, using the historically unrelated account of their rebellion against Moses and Aaron (Num 17:9–15). Few people died, for they were delivered by the 'word' of Aaron's prayer, invoking the covenant promise—a further contrast with the impotence of magic. Aaron's symbolic garments reflected the real power of his covenant-faith; the people needed only to be warned, and not destroyed.

Wis 19:1–27. Annihilation at the Red Sea

The Egyptians were not completely convinced; still in mourning, they decided to pursue the Israelites (Ex 14:5–31). God knew this beforehand; he intended to complete the contrast by destroying them and saving Israel in the Red Sea. The author has already described how the whole of creation works to save God's people (6:24–29); here the exodus symbolically re-enacts the creation (19:8–12). The cloud covered the camp as the Spirit covered the waters (Gen 1:2); dry land appeared from the sea (Gen 1:9–10), covered with vegetation (Gen 1:11–13) and gnats instead of animals, quail (a new bird to them) in place of birds (Ex 1:20). Thunder accompanied the exodus as it did creation (Ps 104:7). They should have been warned by the thunder, which recalls the destruction of Sodom (Gen 19:11–24). The Sodomites were punished for refusing hospitality, a basic law in the East; but the Egyptians had first welcomed the Israelites and then turned on them, a far worse crime. 19:18–21 takes up the previous theme of the role of creation; the author utilises the Greek metaphor of the harmony of the cosmos, to summarise the antitheses. While the melody may change, the basic harmony remains. The Israelite cattle went through the Red Sea, frogs emerged on land in Egypt, fire and water did not cancel each other out, as testimony to God's power. All this proves the unfailing power and presence of God, protecting his people even to the present.

1. Can we in any sense be encouraged by the history of Israel?
2. Is modern Israel a sign of God's covenant-promise?
3. Can we glory in the punishment of the wicked?